GW00659469

THE FIRST WORLD WAR

ARMS and UNIFORMS

Other titles in this series:

Arms and Uniforms 1–Ancient Egypt to the 18th Century

Arms and Uniforms 2–18th Century to the Present Day

The Napoleonic Wars 1

The Napoleonic Wars 2

The First World War 2

THE FIRST WORLD WAR

PART 1
The Infantry of the Allies
and the Central Powers,
Tanks, Aircraft

Liliane and Fred Funcken

WARD LOCK LIMITED · LONDON

© Illustrations Casterman 1970
© Text Ward Lock 1974

ISBN 0 7063 1883 8

First published in Great Britain 1974 by
Ward Lock Limited, 116 Baker Street,
London, W1M 2BB

All Rights Reserved. No part of this
publication may be reproduced, stored
in a retrieval system, or transmitted, in
any form or by any means, electronic,
mechanical, photocopying, recording,
or otherwise, without the prior per-
mission of the Copyright owners.

Designed by Conal Buck

Text filmset in 11/13pt Baskerville
by V. Siviter Smith & Co Ltd

Printed and bound by Casterman,
Tournai, Belgium

Contents

The Allies   10

The Central Powers   94

Armour and Aircraft   122

Acknowledgements   151

List of Sources   153

Index   155

Foreword

In the south-western suburbs of Vienna, there lies the Heeresgeschichtliches Museum, the Austrian Army Museum. Almost the first thing that the visitor comes upon is an enormous motor-car with glistening horns. This is the vehicle in which the heir to the Austrian throne, the Archduke Franz Ferdinand, and his wife were assassinated by a student, Gavrilo Princip, on 28 June 1914, at Sarajevo. Those two deaths led to the sacrifice of nearly 15,000,000 human lives. The shots of a nineteen-year-old murderer touched off the most ferocious, blood-thirsty and most futile war that mankind has ever known.

Our aim in producing this first volume, dealing with the uniforms of the First World War, is not to revive the memory of the horrors of war. Rather, it is to record as accurately as possible the exact appearance of the armies that confronted each other during the four years of pitiless struggle. The details of the military operations have no place here, for these have been the subject of many far more important works. Our aim is to portray the soldier who played his silent, often tragic, part and who, despite the miseries of his surroundings, showed a remarkable ability to survive the worst. At the same time, we hope to explain the purpose and the importance of the more remote theatres of operations and to throw fresh light on the intricacies of the course of events in the Balkans, the Caucasus and the Middle East.

We hope that our readers, in glancing through this volume, will find something to satisfy their curiosity about the soldiers of the First World War, here depicted all together and in detail for the first time.

PART ONE
THE ALLIES

The French Infantry

Any description of the French foot soldier of 1914 must inevitably remind one of the soldiers of the Franco-Prussian War, portrayed in the paintings of Alphonse de Neuville and Edouard Détaille[1], because they were so similar in appearance. Indeed, it needs a sharp eye to detect the slight differences of detail between them like the smaller pack and a magazine rifle.

Like his forbear in 1870, the foot soldier in 1914 wore a cloth *képi* with a canvas body and a leather head-band. The crown was maroon and the band was dark blue for Line Regiments. The whole was dark blue for the *Chasseurs à pied* (Light Infantry).

The greatcoat was dark blue-grey, double-breasted with brass buttons and a waistcoat or a tunic was worn underneath it. The trousers were maroon for Line Regiments and dark blue for the *Chasseurs*. In service dress, these were tucked into laced, black-leather leggings and, in this order of dress, the only other difference was that the *képi* had a blue stuff cover. In addition to a pair of ankle boots, the soldier had a pair of slippers, nicknamed *godillots* after their inventor, which were carried attached to the valise.

This valise, which was known as the 'Azor', is worthy of mention for seldom has any army been given a piece of equipment so badly designed. The 1893-pattern (modified) valise was made of black canvas, and it was made waterproof, in theory at least, by the application of a black substance. This particular version of 'spit and polish' served as a ready form of punishment because the soldier had to go to considerable trouble to bring the valise up to the required standard. Despite their efforts, it was seldom that a day passed without several men being punished for failing to achieve the desired results. One trick was to use boot polish instead of the 'issue' cleaning material but, if it started to rain, the man could not touch his equipment without getting dirty and the water ran down the skirts of his greatcoat in black streams. The short-comings of the valise did not end there: putting it on was a most complicated affair and it took the recruit months to learn to do this single-handed. Even for the experienced it was not easy to do in the excitement of an alarm.

The same may be said of the braces to which the pouches were attached. The pouches were just as unpractical as the valise. They opened from the front, so that the movement of the flap was restricted by the body of the wearer and it kept on falling on his fingers. There was also a third pouch, which was carried on the back of the waist-belt; this had been introduced when the valise of 1893 was made smaller. It is obvious that, on a short man, the valise bore down on the pouch at the back, pressing it against the man's kidneys, which pain eventually became unbearable.

1 Alphonse de Neuville (1836–85) painted *Les Dernieres Cartouches* (Last Man, Last Round); an incident in the defence of Bazeilles, on 1 September 1870. Edouard Detaille (1848–1912) was a military artist, known for his accuracy of detail. Together with Neuville, he painted *The Panorama of the Battle of Champigny,* (Siege of Paris 30 November to 3 December 1870).

FRENCH INFANTRY, 1914

1. Infantry of the Line — 2. *Chasseur à Pied* — 3. Infantry of the Line, with *képi* cover — 4. Bicycle scout — 5. Reservist — 6. Officer with patrol jacket.

The list of the defects and short-comings of the French equipment did not end here. However to conclude, we shall only mention the tool-kit, which consisted of an oil-bottle, a reamer and a flat screwdriver, together weighing a little over half an ounce; their container, which was made to last forever, weighed seven times as much. The towel was removed from the list of necessaries carried in the field which might suggest that, in war, the men gave up washing. Such was not the case, however, for they still carried a piece of soap. A cotton night-cap also remained in the list of necessaries[2].

Several types of mobile field-kitchen were tried out before 1914, but none proved satisfactory. Consequently, most of the time, the French infantry carried on their backs their biscuits and bully, canvas buckets, mess-tins, reserve rations, communal and individual cooking utensils, bags of coffee, salt and sugar, and–for there is nothing like freshly-ground coffee–a coffee-mill per section. Add to this, a bag or so per man containing the day's rations, a mug and a knife and fork.

One cannot but feel a mixture of pity and admiration when one thinks of the *poilu* staggering along in the heat of the August sun of 1914, carrying over 66 lb.

The Rifle

Incorrectly called the 'Lebel' but less conveniently designated *fusil 86 modifié 93* (Rifle, 1886-pattern, modified 1893), this weapon weighed, fully charged, about $9\frac{3}{4}$ lb. This rifle had been developed at Châlons, under the supervision of Colonel Lebel, in 1882. The bolt was modified by the addition of tenons on both sides by Colonel Bonnet; smokeless powder, known as *poudre B* in honour of the famous General Boulanger, was produced by Vieille; the nickel-covered bullet was devised by Colonel Lebel; the Clause magazine was incorporated in the design and finally, Colonel Capdevieille's sword-bayonet, weighing about 1 lb, made its appearance. Thus transformed, the Lebel became a repeating rifle with a calibre of 8 mm (·315 in). There was no

separate magazine and, of the ten rounds it held, eight lay in a tubular magazine in the stock, one in a cavity beneath the breech and one in the breech. This mechanism had the disadvantages that it was heavy, that the centre of gravity was thrown out and that to recharge the magazine was a slow and difficult process. The Lebel was improved in 1893, by the adoption of a new type of round with a brass-covered ball, known as the *balle D* after Desaleux, which was lighter, shorter and reduced the weight of the rifle, without its triangular bayonet, to slightly over 9 lb. This bayonet was the well-known 'Rosalie', the subject of a song by Botrel[3]. We should mention that the bayonet was used far less often than is generally supposed.

THE REGIMENTS

Infantry of the Line

The Infantry of the Line consisted of 173 Regiments, each, when mobilised, of a strength of 73 Officers and 3,200 men[4].

Territorials

After eleven years of reserve liability, the French citizen was transferred to the *territoriale* for seven years[5]. The equipment was the same as that for the Regiments of the Line.

2 This list, which has been shortened, is taken from an exhaustive study by Commander Lavisse, published in Paris in 1903. It does not appear to have had any effect.
3 Theodore Botrel (1868–1925), military song-writer and author of the *Paimpolaise*.
4 Unlike British Infantry Regiments which can consist of any number of Battalions, French Infantry Regiments were always composed of 3 Battalions so that, in effect, it was the same as the Infantry elements in a Brigade.
5 *La Territoriale* was a reserve that has no British equivalent. It was in no way comparable with the Territorial Force which was a volunteer force, originally with a liability for service in Great Britain only.

FRENCH INFANTRY, 1914–15

1–2. The new uniform (1915) — 3. *Chasseur Alpin* (1914) — 4. *Chasseur Alpin* (1915) — 5. *Chasseurs Alpins* (1914) with Hotchkiss machine gun

L. & F. Funcken

Chasseurs à Pied

As we have seen, there was little difference in appearance between the Infantry of the Line and the *Chasseurs à pied* and their equipment was the same. There were 31 Battalions of *Chasseurs*. Nicknamed *vitriers* (glaziers), the *Chasseurs à pied* were raised under Louis-Philippe as the *Chasseurs d'Orléans* and, in 1848, they became the *Chasseurs de Vincennes*.

The *Chasseurs à pied* served with distinction in Algeria, on the Isly, at Sidi-Brahim, at Solferino and in many other places. They were all young men and hand-picked.

Chasseurs Alpins

A number of Battalions of *Chasseurs* were allocated for the defence of the Alpine frontier and were consequently styled *Chasseurs alpins*. They were recruited largely from the inhabitants of the region. They wore bérets with yellow badges in the form of a hunting-horn, blue jackets with fall collars, which were far more comfortable than the stand collar worn by the rest of the Infantry Regiments raised in France, and blue puttees. Their valise, however, was a bit heavier.

Alpine Infantry

The Alpine Infantry were often confused with the *Chasseurs alpins*. They wore the same equipment, but their badge was in the form of a red grenade, and they had red trousers like the Infantry of the Line. They mustered six Regiments.

The Infantry of the Army of Africa and the Colonial Infantry

The Army of Africa consisted of troops raised in Tunisia, Algeria and Morocco. The Colonial Army, in co-operation with the Army of Africa, served alongside the Regiments raised in France in all the great battles of the First World War.

Zouaves

The Zouaves, of whom there were four Regiments, were raised in Algeria by the Duke of Rovigo in 1831. Their strange costume never failed to attract the sightseer.

Tirailleurs

The *Tirailleurs*, nicknamed 'turcos', wore a uniform like that of the Zouaves, but in light blue instead of dark blue. In 1914, they mustered nine Regiments drawn from the various tribes and races of North Africa. By the end of 1915, three more Regiments had been raised.

Tirailleurs Sénégalais

At the outbreak of hostilities, the *Tirailleurs Sénégalais* were wearing single-breasted, navy blue jackets with yellow facings and lace, the titles 'T.S.', dark blue breeches and red fez with blue tassels.

Colonial Infantry

The Colonial Infantry wore a double-breasted tunic and the usual dark blue-grey greatcoat, but with blue trousers with red stripes. The *képi* badge was a red anchor.

The Foreign Legion

The Foreign Legion mobilised at Sidi-bel-Abbès and at Saïda, and sent units to fight in France,

FRENCH INFANTRY:
ARMS, EQUIPMENT AND BADGES, 1914

1. Valise with 'full pack' — 2. Valise without mess-tin — 3. Valise showing construction: (a) Pocket for 'small book' (b) Wooden frame (c) Main compartment — 4. Belt and braces with ammunition pouches and bayonet frog — 5. Folding saw — 6. Entrenching tool (left) and pick-axe — 7. Water-bottle — 8. Mug — 9. Cooking-bowl for eight men — 10. Marching boots — 11. Bugle, Infantry of the Line — 12. *Képi*, Infantry of the Line — 13. *Képi, Chasseurs à Pied* — 14. Lebel rifle, 1886–93-pattern, with diagram showing method of operation of the magazine — 15. Bayonet and scabbard — 16. Marksman's badge, Infantry of the Line and Zouaves — 17. Best Shot (gold or silver, matching the buttons) — 18. Marksman's badge, *Chasseurs à Pied, Tirailleurs Algériens* and African Light Infantry — 19. Bandsman — 20. Bomber (also in blue) — 21. Chief armourer — 22. Signaller — 23. Pioneer — 24. Machine-gunner — 25. Cyclist

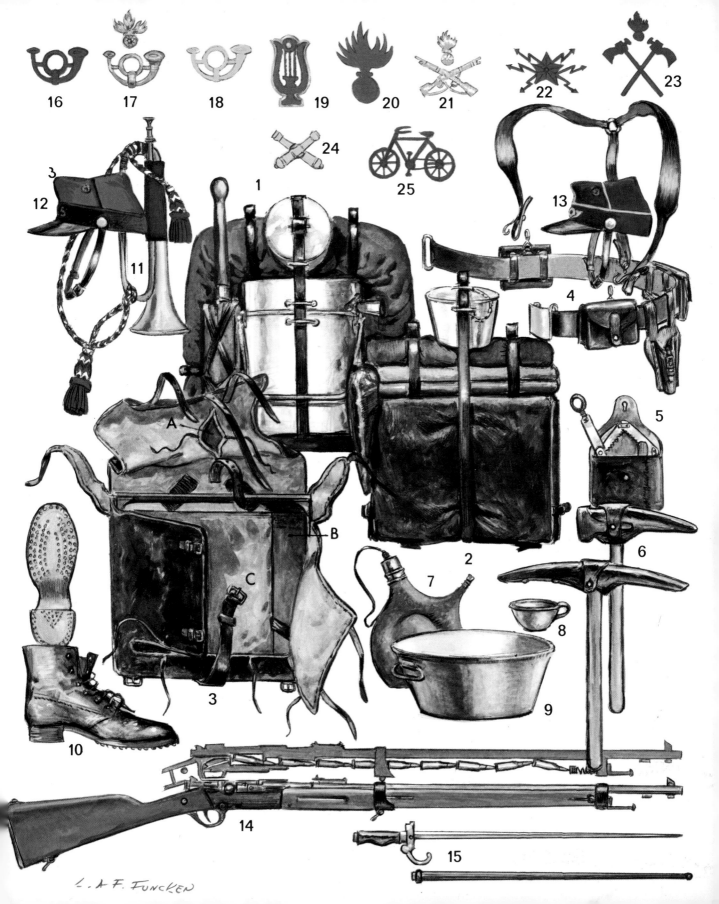

16 17 18 19 20 21 22 23

24 25

3 12 11 1 13 4

A 5

B

C 6

10 3 7 8 2

9

14

15

L. A. F. FUNCKEN

where they saw action in October 1914. It goes without saying that care was taken to keep legionaries from Germany and Austria in Africa. The uniform of the Foreign Legion was the same as that of the Regiments of the Line.

The amalgamation of different detachments, some from Africa, others formed from volunteers of all nationalities in France, resulted in the creation of the famous *régiments de marche* culminating in the even more renowned *régiment de marche de la Légion étrangère* formed in 1915. There were the following *régiments de marche*:

1st Regiment, Foreign Legion–

2nd Regiment: 1 September 1914 to 11 November 1915;

3rd Regiment: 1 September 1914 to 13 August 1915, when it was amalgamated with the 2nd Regiment;

4th Regiment (Garibaldians): 5 November 1914 to May 1915, when it returned to Italy; and

2nd Regiment, Foreign Legion–

2nd Regiment: 1 September 1914 to 11 November 1915.

The *régiment de marche de la Légion étrangère* was formed on 11 November 1915 from the two 2nd Regiments named above. It returned to Africa in March 1919 and was reformed as the 3rd Regiment, Foreign Legion in 1920.

Early in 1915, the Foreign Legion adopted the horizon blue uniform. Then, with the formation of the *régiment de marche de la Légion étrangère* in November 1915, it changed to khaki.

TRENCH WARFARE

We have described briefly the uniform and equipment of the foot soldier who marched off to war in the August of 1914, encouraged by the cheers of the crowd and determined to 'bring back the Kaiser's moustache'. All ranks were convinced that a bayonet charge was the answer to a dug-in enemy. Blinded by a superiority complex, the French were unable to see the weakness of their strategy. For example, on 22 August 1914 before Châtelet in Belgium, in a matter of minutes the 1st Algerian *Tirailleurs* lost 1,034 men charging an invisible enemy. On the same day, the same thing happened to the 3rd Division of the Colonial Infantry in the valley of the Semois.

On a bigger scale, the 5th Army incurred losses on 21, 22 and 23 August and was only saved at the last minute by the exertions of General Lanzerac.

Then came the retreat, for there was no other way of escaping annihilation at the hands of the German Army. The smart men of August had become a subdued and ragged band, their condition worsened by the weather, burning sun alternating with torrential rain. Nevertheless, they fell back to the Marne in good order and there General Joffre, with the help of General Gallieni and the famous 'Marne taxis' which brought up 7,000 reinforcements, broke the German advance in September 1914.

After the Battles of the Somme (20–30 September), the Yser (15 October–3 November) and Ypres (30 October–11 November), where the German 7th Infantry Division lost 80% of its strength, all hope of an early victory vanished. Realising that neither side could triumph over the other, both sides dug in and settled down in hastily constructed trenches behind a tangle of barbed wire.

The war of the trenches, that was to bring long years of suffering amidst mud, rats and fleas, had started. Not only had the manner of warfare changed, but the men themselves were no longer the same. Their outlook had become conditioned to the prospect of the long struggle to the death that

FRENCH INFANTRY:
ARMY OF AFRICA, 1914–15

1. Zouave with cotton overalls (1914–15) — 2. Zouave (1915) — 3. St Étienne machine gun, 1907-pattern — 4. Puteaux machine gun, 1905-pattern — 5. Algerian *Tirailleur* with cotton jacket and overalls, as Fig. 2 — 6. Algerian *Tirailleur* with cotton overalls (1914–15) — 7. Moroccan *Tirailleur* — 8. Foreign Legion — 9. Algerian *Tirailleur* in new uniform (1915)

was just beginning. Two photographs, taken within a few months of each other, are particularly revealing. One, taken in September 1914, shows the graves of the French soldiers around Barcy, each with its flowers and its little French flag. The other, taken in February 1915, shows a French trench that has just been retaken and the counter-attackers, with self-satisfied smiles, are standing behind the piled corpses of their comrades in arms which are awaiting burial in a common grave. There is no sentimentality now. Horrors have become commonplace and this, perhaps, is the true picture of war.

In the mind of the French soldier, these trenches were not destined to be occupied for long because the formidable Russian Army would intervene and this would allow the Allies[6] to resume the offensive. However, that was not how things turned out and the soldiers had to resign themselves to digging more and more trenches, parallels, communication trenches and dug-outs, all in the most appalling conditions.

HOW THE UNIFORM DEVELOPED

As may be imagined, the uniform had proved a disaster in the trenches, particularly the red trousers. By the end of 1914, blue cotton overalls had been issued to hide them. These were soon replaced by corduroy trousers of a strange sort. In order to give these navvies' garments a more martial appearance, a bright yellow stripe, which was to become the mark of the infantry, was put down the side. There is a story, in this context, of an old soldier who was wearing a pair of beige corduroys that his mother had sent him. His Company Commander ordered him not to wear them because they had no stripe and, if he were taken prisoner, he would run the risk of being shot as a *franc-tireur*.

The Horizon-blue Uniform

The famous horizon-blue uniform was introduced in April 1915[7]. The weave was three-coloured; 35% white wool, 15% dark blue wool and 50% light blue wool. In the summer of 1915, the Colonial Troops adopted khaki.

The regimental numeral was in gold for the officers and in silver for the non-commissioned officers. At this time, the marks of rank on the *képi* were discontinued and those on the cuffs were reduced in length to a little under $1\frac{1}{2}$ in.

By the end of 1915, the use of silver numerals to distinguish the non-commissioned officers had been discontinued and that metal, once again, became the distinctive metal for the cavalry.

Finally, the following identifications evolved:

Branch	Collar Patch	Soutache[8] and Regimental Numeral
Infantry of the Line	Bright yellow	Dark blue
Chasseurs à pied	Blue-grey	Bright yellow
Colonial Infantry	Bright yellow	Bright yellow

6 The Allies were the countries fighting against Germany, Austria-Hungary, Bulgaria, and Turkey, who were collectively known as the Central Powers.

7 In 1911, a mignonette-green (reseda) uniform was considered at the request of the Minister for War, M. Berteaux, but was rejected as being too ugly.

8 *Soutache* is the name of the little chevrons forming the trimming at the rear of the collar patch. See page 13, 2.

FRENCH INFANTRY:
COLONIAL TROOPS AND COLONIAL INFANTRY, 1914–15

1. Colonial Infantry, Private (1914) — 2. Colonial Infantry, Corporal (1914) — 3. Tonkinese *Tirailleur* (1914) (later they wore horizon-blue and a beret) — 4. Senegalese *Tirailleur* — 5. Senegalese *Tirailleur*, battle order, with cover to fez — 6. Senegalese *Tirailleur*, summer dress

Although in theory the trouser stripe of the infantry was bright yellow, in the pressure of business, the depots issued artillery trousers with red stripes to the infantry and vice versa, so that the outcome was that the stripes were forgotten and the leg-wear became plain horizon-blue for all. Originally the equipment had been black, but now it was being issued undyed so that young soldiers were dubbed 'yellow braces' (*bretelles jaunes*).

The bright yellow collar patch did not last long; an amendment in May 1915 altered the colour to horizon-blue but did not abolish the collar patch as such.

The Steel Helmet

With the new uniform, there appeared also the first steel helmet for the infantry, known as the 'Adrian helmet' after the Stores Officer who devised it. The basis was a disc of cold-forged steel about 13 in in diameter and $\frac{1}{32}$ in thick. From this, the body of the helmet was formed and a crest and a brim were riveted to it. There were three sizes weighing, on an average, $1\frac{1}{2}$ lb. The helmet was painted a blue-grey, known as artillery grey, the same colour as the well-known 'French 75' gun.

This helmet bore a distinctive badge according to the arm of the service: a granade for the Infantry of the Line, a hunting-horn for the *Chasseurs,* an anchor for the Colonial Infantry, a helmet and cuirass for the Engineers and crossed guns for the Artillery. Photographs show that the Artillery, in practice, also wore the grenade.

Before the appearance of the Adrian helmet, there had been a metal crown to be worn inside the *képi,* but these uncomfortable objects were used as cooking utensils as often as not.

The Fourragère

Fourragère is the name given to the ornamental plaited cord terminating in a brass tag worn at the shoulder in uniform by all ranks of certain units of the Army that have been commended for their distinguished conduct in action. Similar awards are also made to the Navy and to the Air Force. To qualify for the award, which was instituted in 1915, a unit must, in normal circumstances, have received two 'citations' (roughly, the equivalent of a Mention in Despatches) in Army Orders. There are, at the present time, five different *fourragères*: *Croix de Guerre,* 1914–18 (green and red); *Croix de Guerre,* 1939–45 (green and red, but different from the preceding); *Croix de Guerre des Théatres d'Opérations Extérieurs* (T.O.E.), that is, operations overseas other than in the two World Wars (rose and pale blue); *Médaille Militaire* (yellow and green); and *Légion d'Honneur* (scarlet).

During the Great War of 1914–18, the *fourragère* of the *Croix de Guerre* was awarded for two citations; that of the *Médaille Militaire* for four; and that of the *Légion d'Honneur* for six. For nine or more citations, two *fourragères* were awarded: those of the *Légion d'Honneur* and the *Croix de Guerre* for nine; those of the *Légion d'Honneur* and the *Médaille Militaire* for twelve; and two of the *Légion d'Honneur* for fifteen.

The *fourragère* of the *Croix de Guerre* T.O.E. was instituted 'between the wars' and is worn separate-

FRENCH INFANTRY, 1916–18

1. Foot soldier in battle order, with 1907–15-pattern rifle, and bayonet with steel hilt without quillon — 2. Officer, *Chasseurs à Pied* — 3. Bugler — 4. Bugler, with helmet cover — 5–6. Look-out, with periscope — 7. Gas alarm
Fourragères: 8. *Croix de Guerre,* two or three citations — 9. *Médaille Militaire,* four or five citations — 10. *Légion d'Honneur,* six to eight citations — 11. *Croix de Guerre* and *Légion d'Honneur,* nine to eleven citations — 12. *Médaille Militaire* and *Légion d'Honneur,* twelve to fourteen citations — 13. *Légion d'Honneur,* fifteen or more citations — 14. Details of the plaits: (a) *Croix de Guerre* 1914–18 (b) *Médaille Militaire* (c) *Légion d'Honneur* — 15. Manner of wearing in walking-out dress — 16. Examples of 'olives': (a) *Croix de Guerre* (b) *Médaille Militaire* and *Croix de Guerre* (c) *Légion d'Honneur* and *Croix de Guerre* (d) *Légion d'Honneur, Croix de Guerre* T.O.E. and *Croix de Guerre* (e) *Légion d'Honneur, Médaille Militaire* and *Croix de Guerre* — 17. Section of a F1 Grenade

ly, unless the Regiment to which it is awarded already has the *fourragère* of the *Médaille Militaire* or a higher award, when an 'olive' in its colours is placed on the cord of the latter above the tag.

Likewise, in the Second World War, when a new *fourragère* for the *Croix de Guerre* was introduced in April 1939, all regiments started from scratch. The qualifications required were the same as in the Great War but, if a unit already had a *fourragère*, use was again made of the 'olive'. Only the superior grade of *fourragère* is worn. Thus, if a regiment with the *fourragère* of the *Médaille Militaire* from the Great War, gained one of the *Croix de Guerre* in the Second World War, they would put the 'olive' of the *Croix de Guerre* on the cord of the *fourragère* of the *Médaille Militaire*. A regiment that had the *fourragère* of the *Croix de Guerre* from the Great War, upon achieving the same honour in the Second World War, would have worn the 'olive' of the *Croix de Guerre*, 1939–45 but, on subsequently attaining to the *Médaille Militaire* or the *Légion d'Honneur*, would wear the 'olive' of the *Croix de Guerre*, 1914–18 on the appropriate *fourragère*.

Citations are not additive; a regiment that had three from the Great War, upon gaining one in the Second World War, did not qualify for the *fourragère* of the *Médaille Militaire* as a result.

The only exception to the rules regarding the numbers of citations required to qualify for the award of a *fourragère*, was that a unit which captured a standard, guidon or colour from the enemy was granted the *fourragère* of the *Légion d'Honneur*. This, however, is really academic as these flags have not been carried in battle for almost a century.

THE DEVELOPMENT OF THE WEAPONS

Grenades

With the coming of trench-warfare, extra weapons were invented or re-appeared, one of the latter being the grenade. The need for grenades became so great that antiquated grenades of cast-iron ignited by a match, which were known as Sebastopol grenades, and a sea-service type ignited by friction were unearthed from the arsenals. This latter was thrown by means of a sling attached to a striker which was inserted into the grenade, the act of throwing withdrew it and so struck the match. The fuse was set at four seconds, which gave time for the grenade to be thrown back whence it had come.

As neither of these types of grenade proved satisfactory, the men in the fighting line set about devising others. One of these was the *raquette* (racket), which consisted of a wooden pallet to which a charge of melinite was tied or a jam tin containing rusty nails and a charge of cheddite. This device was set off by a slow fuse ignited by the current form of pipe-lighter or a match. This makeshift projectile, which was also called a *calendrier* (calendar), often proved as dangerous to its own side as it did to the enemy.

By the end of 1915, improved grenades were appearing, offensive, defensive, incendiary, and asphyxiating. The best-known were:
1. The *C.F. défensive*, which consisted of an ovoid, segmented cast-iron body which fragmented on explosion. To prime this, one removed the white-metal cap protecting the percussion-cap and then knocked in the wooden striker[9] against something hard.

2. The *O.F. offensive*, which had a plain white-metal body, was not effective at over 5 yards, and could be thrown by an unprotected man in the open. It weighed about 10 oz and was operated in the same manner as the *C.F. défensive*.

9 The story that this was done against the hilt of the bayonet is one of those picturesque details thought up after the War. This grenade was only used at short range when the bayonet would be fixed, not in the scabbard.

FRENCH INFANTRY:
ASSAULT TROOPS, 1917–18

1. Machine-gunners and bombers — 2. Light infantry and bombers with rifles fitted with dischargers — 3. Bombers and 'mopping-up' sections — 4. Reinforcements — 5. Chauchat light machine gun (called a Chauchard by the British and Shosho by the Americans)

3. The *F1 défensive,* which was cast-iron, ovoid and fragmented on explosion, weighed slightly under 1½ lb. On pulling the safety pin, a lever was released. Then, when the grenade was thrown, the lever in turn set free a striker which ignited the charge. This pattern of grenade was introduced in 1916.

4. The 1916-pattern incendiary and smoke grenade consisted of two smooth white-metal halves soldered together.

5. The 'V.B. grenade', named after its inventor, Captain Viven-Bessières, was launched by means of a cup attached to the muzzle of the rifle. The grenade was made of cast-iron and weighed about 13 oz, of which the explosive represented about 2 oz. It was shaped like a doughnut and had a hole through it that was slightly smaller than the bore of the rifle. When the rifle was fired, the bullet shot the grenade into the air, priming it at the same time. The projectile was timed to go off at seven seconds, the range, varying according to the angle of fire, going up to 200 yards. To prove effective, the V.B. grenade required considerable skill on the part of the firer.

Various other machines were devised, such as the *sauterelle* (grasshopper), a sort of cross-bow which had a range of about 80 yards.

Rifles and Machine Guns[10]

The Lebel rifle was retained but another, the 1907–15-pattern with a three-round charger, was also brought into service. This latter, which had been developed from the 1907-pattern rifle, was known as the 'Senegal' or the 'Colonial' and was issued to the newest recruits. This rifle was modified again in 1916 when a five-round charger was introduced.

The Puteaux and the Saint-Étienne machine-guns, which could not stand up to dust and mud, had been replaced by the 1914 Hotchkiss. Although this last had a slower rate of fire (400–450 a minute), it was far more suited to trench warfare[11].

TACTICS

Eventually it was realised that, in static warfare, the infantry alone could not capture ground held by a well dug-in enemy. In 1914, the French artillery was inadequate, but it was quickly improved and adapted to co-operate closely with the infantry in the assault by firing preparatory barrages which, it had at last been realised, were essential[12].

The infantry company had evolved too. In 1914, it had comprised 250 riflemen and shared a machine gun with another company. By 1917 however, the strength had dropped to 194 men, but armed both with V.B. rifles and light machine guns[13] and supported by a battalion gun of 37 mm[14].

The infantry company attacked with the light machine gunners and the bombers in front, well spread out to minimise casualties. Next came the rifle sections and these were followed by the 'cleaners-up' (*nettoyeurs*) who cleared any survivors of the attack out of the trenches. Then came the reinforcements in a solid body, whose job was to consolidate the ground gained. Eventually, the *poilu*[15], fighting on and on, won through by sheer endurance.

10 See also pages 42 and 62.
11 Trench Artillery will be dealt with in Volume II in the chapter on Artillery.
12 The Artillery are dealt with in Volume II.
13 See the section on the American Expeditionary Forces.
14 See Volume II.
15 *Poilu* is the French equivalent of 'Tommy' in the British Army. It meant hairy; the French privates did not shave on active service.

FRENCH INFANTRY:
ARMY OF AFRICA AND COLONIAL TROOPS

1. Hotchkiss machine gun, 1914-pattern, on a 1910-pattern tripod — 2. Hotchkiss machine gun, 1900-pattern — 3. Moroccan *Tirailleur* (1918) — 4. Battalion Colour-bearer, Mixed Regiment of Zouaves and *Tirailleurs* (1917–18) — 5. Foreign Legion (1918) — 6. Bugler, Foreign Legion (1918) — 7. Foreign Legion (1915)

The Belgian Infantry

Three soldiers of the Allies were chatting together, so the story goes, and the French *poilu* said to the British Tommy, 'What do you want written on your wooden cross?' 'Died for His Majesty.' replied the Tommy 'And what about you?' 'Died for France.' said the Frenchman, adding to the Belgian 'And you?' 'Didn't want to die.' replied the Belgian.

This story originated in Belgium, for private circulation, but has been used by military writers, generally abusively, to illustrate the prosaic outlook of the Belgian soldier of 1914–18. If the outlook of the men who fought so ferociously at Liége, Namur, Antwerp, and Dixmude, was so narrow, one wonders how they managed to show the immense courage which excited the admiration of the whole world at the time.

The Belgian infantrymen of 1914, and indeed the soldiers of the other arms too, had something of a comic opera appearance. The shiny hats of the *carabiniers* and the stiff shakos of the Line, the dark green or dark blue uniforms and the glinting brass all helped to make the Belgian soldier an easy target.

On service, the grenadiers replaced their bear-skins by pill-boxes. For everyone, the pack was made of rawhide and the big ammunition pouch was of black leather. The rifle was the German Mauser with a five-round magazine, 1889-pattern. The calibre was 7·65 mm. The length without the bayonet, was nearly 4 ft 2 in and it weighed almost 9¾ lb. It was an excellent weapon, the first of the modern Mauser type.

The War came just as the Belgian Army was being reorganised. Up to 1909, the army had been composed largely of volunteers, with a small number of conscripts found by ballot. The latter, however, could always escape military service by paying for a substitute. The laws regarding military service, that came into force in 1909, abolished this somewhat unfair system and substituted service by one of the sons of each family, while retaining the voluntary service for those who wished to make the army their career. Then by a law passed on 28 March 1913, compulsory military service was introduced.

The 5th edition of the Infantry Manual (*Manual d'instruction théorique pour le soldat d'infanterie*), revised and re-issued in 1912, reveals that the army staff of the time had a very poor opinion of the mental capacity of the conscripts or maybe they were simply being realistic. This curious work took the form of a catechism, explaining by question and answer everything the soldier should know about his uniform, how and whom to salute, discipline, leave, pay, etc. There are also questions such as, 'Who is your King? Your Queen? What is the capital of Belgium? What are the colours of the Belgian flag? What is the shape of the earth? What are cross-roads? What do you understand by a clearing? By a spring? What is a main road? A milestone? A path?' The prize, however, goes to 'Q. How can you tell a bad soldier? A. A bad soldier is one who is despondent, who does not look after his feet and his footwear and who deserts in time of stress.'

The Belgian infantry had a mobilisation strength of between 85,000 and 93,000; 60,000 of which were reservists. The twenty regiments, unsatisfactorily reorganised into the same number of mixed brigades, had too small a regular cadre. There were fourteen Line Regiments, three of *Chasseurs-à-pied*, two of *Carabiniers* and one of Grenadiers.

Several different types of machine-guns had

BELGIAN INFANTRY, 1914

1. H.M. King Albert I of the Belgians, in service dress — 2. *Chasseur à Pied* — 3. *Carabinier* — 4. General Officer — 5. Corporal, Grenadiers — 6–7. Infantry of the Line

been tried and their varying merits had been discussed for years; however at the outbreak of war the Belgian Army had only one hundred and twelve Maxims and about fifty Hotchkiss, obviously quite insufficient.

THE ORIGINS OF THE VARIOUS REGIMENTS

Infantry of the Line

The Line Regiments dated from the Revolution of 1830, when the regiments from Brussels, Namur, Mons, Tournai, Maastricht, Bruges and etc, were numbered from 1 to 11 as Regiments of the Line. A 12th was raised in 1831 and the 13th and 14th in 1870.

Carabiniers

The *Carabiniers* were descended from two partisan units, one from Limbourg and the other from Flanders, who had distinguished themselves in the struggle against Holland and had been amalgamated with the 1st *Chasseurs à Pied* in 1834. The regiment got its name from the Delvigne-Ponchara carbine with which it was issued in 1837. At first, the regiment were known as *Chasseurs Carabiniers*, but the title was changed in 1850 to *Carabiniers*.

In 1898, a number of cyclist companies were raised, these were formed into an independent corps in 1914. The cyclists distinguished themselves in their early encounters with the invaders in 1914, to the extent that the Germans nicknamed them The Black Devils (*Schwarze Teufel*).

Chasseurs à Pied

As we have seen, the 1st *Chasseurs à Pied* were converted into *Chasseurs Carabiniers* in 1837. A new 1st Regiment was raised in 1874, but the 2nd and 3rd Regiments had been in existence since 1831.

Grenadiers

The Grenadiers received their colour in 1837, and were granted the title *Régiment d'Élite* two years later. Upon the outbreak of the Great War, a second regiment was formed and the two were numbered the 1st and 2nd Regiments, but their losses were so heavy that they were amalgamated in November 1914. In 1916 however, the Grenadiers were again formed into two regiments.

Gendarmerie à Pied

After the Revolution of 1830, the forces of law and order that had joined the Provisional Government were given the title Belgian National Gendarmerie (*Gendarmerie Nationale Belge*). A Royal Decree in 1832 established their uniform, which has retained its main features even to the present time[16].

BELGIUM IN THE WAR

At Visé, on 4 August 1914, six *gendarmes* fired the first shots and stood firm until they were annihilated by the onslaught of the soldiers of the Kaiser.

The invasion carried on. A desperate telegram was sent from Verviers, a textile town close to the German frontier, which read 'The Germans are at the gates!' Immediately, some reservists started making their way cautiously along the railway cutting between Verviers and Liége in an attempt to reach the fortifications of the latter town.

The strong point of Liége comprised twelve forts which, the Belgian High Command were well aware, could only serve to check the enemy's advance. The Belgian Army consisted of six

16 See Volume II.

BELGIAN INFANTRY, 1914–15

1. Foot soldier (1914–15) — 2. Foot soldier with velvet breeches (1914–15) — 3. Machine-gunner, wearing the first type of gas-mask which had no filter — 4. Foot soldier (1914–15) — 5. Original khaki uniform (Spring 1915)

BELGIAN INFANTRY, 1914

1. Cyclist machine-gunners, *Carabiniers* — 2. Cyclist Battalion, *Carabiniers* — 3. Maxim machine gun, drawn by dog team — 4. Maxim machine gun team, *Carabiniers*

L. & F. Funcken

4

divisions[17] each of three or four mixed infantry brigades, three artillery groups and one cavalry regiment. The 3rd Division, reinforced by a brigade from the 4th Division, was based on Liége and, including the garrison troops, there were some 47,500 troops to oppose the 55,000 Germans who were supported by a large amount of heavy artillery. Although the defenders enjoyed initial success, the 3rd Division was ordered to fall back on the main body of the army on 6 August, too soon as it turned out, because of bad intelligence. The forts continued to put up an heroic resistance on their own until 15 August[18]. The advance had been checked: the Germans did not take Huy and Ardenne until 17 and 19 August respectively. The same thing happened at Namur, where the 4th Division was, as at Liége.

Under the prudent leadership of King Albert I, the Belgian Army withdrew in good order and, to avoid being surrounded by the ever-increasing numbers of German troops, fell back on Antwerp.

The strong point of Antwerp, believed impregnable, was looked upon as the national stronghold, the last ditch. The complex, which was world-famous, with its entrenched camp measured 25 miles from north to south and 17 miles from east to west. The whole army was concentrated there, except for the 4th Division which had fallen back from Namur to Rouen.

In a month, the whole character of the army had changed, starting with the officers whose gaudy uniforms had served to draw the enemy's fire. The men, too, soon discovered the dangers of their shakos of shiny material and quickly painted them a matt colour or, as a last resort, rubbed them with mud. The fatigue caps, too easy to see with their red bands, were turned inside out and all attempts at smartness were forgotten. Thousands of volunteers, all in the highest spirits, came forward, mostly still wearing plain clothes.

Antwerp had but a short respite. It soon became only too clear that the 'impregnable stronghold', poorly armed and unfinished, was simply a trap where the Germans could lock up and then massacre the exhausted Belgian Army with impunity. Nevertheless, two determined sorties were made on 25 August and on 9 September, these forced the Germans to divert several divisions from the main front on the Marne and the Aisne.

Having decided to put an end to all resistance, the Germans attacked Antwerp with a force of 120,000 men, at the same time bombarding the forts with heavy artillery. The battle lasted from 1 to 6 October, the Belgians being supported by a force of 2,000 British Royal Marines. In the end, retreat was inevitable. Those who got away were in tatters, their regiments reduced to battalions, but they rallied round their King who remained calm and collected. This was on 9 September 1914.

The army, 58,000 strong of which 5,000 were cavalry, consolidated on the Yser, which King Albert declared would be the last line of defence in Belgium and would be held to the last man. This was the start of the Battle of the Yser, a battle unlike anything that had ever before been imagined. For six days and six nights in heavy rain and under continuous artillery fire, the Belgians, reinforced by 3,000 French Marines of the Ronarc'h Brigade[19], known as 'the girls with the red pompoms' (*les demoiselles au pompom rouge*), repulsed the repeated heavy attacks of the German infantry, as many as fifteen times during the night of 23–24 October. The survivors must have been overjoyed when they saw the French 42nd Infantry Division under General Grossetti and a British Army Corps coming to their assistance.

17 As a result of the heavy losses in the first three months, the mixed brigades were abolished and the regiments reformed.
18 See Volume II.
19 See Volume II. The French Marines were dressed like sailors. The French man-o'-war cap is soft and has a red pompom on top so it looks rather like a tam-o'-shanter, a type of woman's hat; hence the German nickname.

BELGIAN INFANTRY, 1914–18: I

1. Lieutenant-General, wearing greatcoat (1918) — 2. Lieutenant-General (1918) — 3. Foot soldier (1917–18) — 4. Service dress (August 1917) — 5. Winter dress (1917–18) — 6. Army Chaplain (1914–15) — 7. Look-out with experimental helmet (1918) — 8. Browning machine gun (U.S.A.) — 9. Chaplain's badge — 10. Lieutenant-General's shoulder-cord (Cf. Fig. 2)

The battle lasted until 3 November, thanks to the heroism of the defenders, and it was only brought to an end when, with the assistance of an old lock-keeper, Charles Louis Kogge and a boatman, Henri Geeraert, the no-man's-land was flooded in the region of the Noord Vaart, halting the enemy's advance.

The price of victory was high: 20,000 Belgian casualties of whom 11,000 were killed. The 7th, 8th, 11th and 12th Regiments of the Line, the 2nd *Carabiniers* and the Grenadiers suffered the greatest losses. Among the Grenadiers who fell was their well-loved commanding officer, Major Count Henri d'Oultremont, an officer who lived up to the highest traditions of his title[20].

THE BELGIAN SOLDIER

The Infantry Manual and its silly questions was a thing of the past and the uniform that it described was soon to be forgotten as well. The Belgian soldier, who liked to keep abreast of his French brothers in arms, considered it an honour to look like them, not only in wearing uniforms that had been supplied by the French but, which was an even greater compliment, in trimming their beards *à la chasseur à pied*. The 1914 call-up wore French uniforms and equipment.

When khaki was introduced, one might have hoped for a uniform as smart as that of the British Army, but the *jass*[21] soon put paid to any such hopes. The jackets soon lost their shape, and bore little resemblance to the elegant Tommies. The leather leggings had been replaced by puttees, which were often made from shrouds, old sacks or even curtains.

The French-pattern helmet painted khaki, with its sour-faced lion's-mask crest proved unpopular. Some livened it up by painting the lion's eyes, which gave it an air of ferocity, but also furnished the German snipers with a mark. Following the example of the French, the Belgians made covers for the helmets and painted them with various badges, fitted them with chin-straps and so on.

The uniforms, originally canvas, were replaced by ones of cloth and the rawhide packs gave place to ones of webbing. The heavy ammunition pouch also gave way to ones of the French and British patterns. There were numerous patterns of water-bottle, some were the blue-enamelled iron British type, some French. Despite general disapproval, the puttees were replaced by frightful little leather anklets, the natural off-spring of the objects worn in 1914.

There was an increase in the proportion of machine-guns and light machine-guns, as well as other support weapons.

In 1918, the infantry was reorganised into divisions, each of three regiments. At this time, a company was 180 strong including all ranks with nine light machine-guns (French Chauchat-pattern) and twelve grenade-dischargers. In each platoon, there were two bomber sections.

On 27 September 1918, the veteran *jass* skirted the flooded area and marched forth towards the final encounter. Side by side with the *poilus* under General Desgouttes and the Tommies under General Plumer, they recaptured Flanders and drove the disorganised enemy eastwards.

The Ceasefire for the Armistice sounded as they neared the gates of Ghent. As a mark of esteem, after the war, the King allowed the infantry to use the Crown as its particular badge.

20 The French *Bulletin des armees de la Republique*, roughly Army Orders, discounts the sacrifices made by the Belgians and attributes the victory exclusively to the French.
21 *Jass* is derived from the Flemish *jas*, a jacket, and is the Belgian equivalent of Tommy and *poilu*.

BELGIAN INFANTRY, 1914–18: II

1–3. Military Foot Police — 4. Officer, Security Forces, Belgian Congo — 5–7. Native troops, Belgian Congo — 8. Web equipment — 9. Order of Leopold I, 5th Class, Military Division — 10. Military Medal, 2nd Class — 11. Military Cross, 2nd Class — 12. *Croix de Guerre* — 13. Order of the Crown of Belgium, 5th Class — 14. Collar badge, Infantry Officer — 15. Cap badge, Infantry Officer

The Armies of the British Empire

King Edward VII succeeded his illustrious mother, who had guided the destiny of the British Empire for sixty-four years, in 1901. He was outspokenly pro-French and, in 1903, signed the *Entente Cordiale*. He was not taken in by the blusterings of his nephew, the Kaiser Wilhelm II[22] whose plans for overseas expansion were only too obvious.

Faced with the arms race in which France, Germany, Austria and Russia competed, Great Britain organised an Expeditionary Force of 160,000 men, without resorting to conscription. King George V continued his father's policy of friendship with France. Coupled with the Irish Troubles which reappeared in 1913, the new King found himself in a very serious situation when war broke out in 1914. In 1917, the Royal Family dropped the name Saxe-Coburg-Gotha in favour of that of Windsor[23].

Not having taken part in any European War since the Crimean War of 1854–56, Great Britain reluctantly joined in and soon took a major part in the conflict. On the evening of the day that Belgium was invaded, the British Ambassador in Berlin delivered a note to the German Chancelry that Great Britain had declared war on Germany.

In Britain, there was general indignation and tens of thousands of volunteers came forward in answer to Lord Kitchener's appeal, made on 8 August, when as War Minister he had called for 100,000 men to reinforce the British Army. It is seldom in history that men have shown such enthusiasm: in one year, 2,000,000 joined the colours. All the same, when Field Marshal French landed on the continent with 100,000 men in August 1914, he had to do what he could with the inadequate forces available to him. Although called by the Germans a contemptible little army[24], the British Expeditionary Force was excellently trained and equipped. It had been mobilised in record time, in an orderly manner and without need for improvisation, and its landing in France was greeted with acclamation.

THE BRITISH INFANTRY

In 1914, a British infantry division consisted of 18,073 of all ranks, 5,592 horses, 76 guns and 24 machine-guns. Throughout the Great War, the British element in Europe kept the name British Expeditionary Force (B.E.F.).

22 Edward VII's eldest sister, the German Empress Victoria, was the mother of Kaiser Wilhelm II.
23 Queen Victoria, of the House of Hanover, had married Prince Albert of Saxe-Coburg-Gotha in 1840.
24 The nickname, the Old Contemptibles, was adopted by the veterans of the Great War.

BRITISH INFANTRY: FULL DRESS

1. Coldstream Guards — 2. Welsh Guards — 3. Drummer, Grenadier Guards — 4. Ensign, Coldstream Guards — 5. Scots Guards — 6. Grenadier Guards — 7. Cap badge, Scots Guards — 8. Cap badge, Coldstream Guards — 9. Cap badge, Grenadier Guards — 10. Unknown badge, said to be Welsh Guards

The Uniform of the Infantry

Since 1905, the British soldier had worn a khaki uniform consisting of a jacket with a stand-and-fall collar and outside pockets, trousers, puttees and a cap with a cloth peak.

The Rifle

Great care had been taken to ensure that the fire-power should be as great as possible. The answer was found in the Lee-Enfield Mark III Rifle, which had a magazine. Although it was only 3 ft 8½ in long, it was rifled in such a way that the ·303 in, cylindro-ogival ball had a muzzle velocity of 734 yards per second. It weighed 8 lb 10½ oz and had the advantage that it could be stripped for cleaning by hand. Its most obvious advantage was the magazine which held ten rounds, contained in two chargers. The regular foot soldier of the B.E.F. was trained to get fifteen rounds a minute on the target.

The German infantry, advancing in close order against the British positions on the Mons Canal on 23 August 1914, were decimated by the 'rapid fire' and believed that the British were using light machine-guns or, at any rate, automatic rifles.

The Equipment

The web equipment, 1908-pattern, which replaced the uncomfortable leather equipment with the heavy cartridge-pouches, was more sensibly constructed so that the cartridge-pockets, the haversack, the water-bottle, the entrenching-tool and the bayonet were easy to reach. Generally, the equipment was of a greenish colour, but in some corps it was made buff or white. The brass mountings were dulled on service to prevent their glinting and giving away positions to the enemy.

The arrangement of the ten cartridge-pockets is worth noting: they were set, five on each side and two over three, attached to the waist-belt in such a position as to leave the arms free. A similar equipment, but of leather, was worn by some units. The valise was worn on the back, steadied by two straps. In some orders of dress, the haversack was worn on the back instead of the valise.

The Bayonet, the Entrenching-Tool and the Water-Bottle

In order to make up for the comparative shortness of the rifle, the bayonet had to be lengthened. The entrenching-tool handle was strapped to the side of the bayonet scabbard. The entrenching-tool blade was carried at the back in a carrier attached to the waist-belt and suspended over the hips.

The water-bottle was made of blue-enamelled iron and covered with brown felt. As this could be removed, specimens are to be found without covers.

Head-Dresses

The cloth-peaked cap was not the only head-dress worn. Although photographs showing it are rare, there was also a cap with ear-flaps, similar to those worn by French and Belgian foresters and peasants, that was described as a 'cap, winter, service dress' in 1915 but became known as the 'cap, soft, service dress' in 1917.

BRITISH INFANTRY: SERVICE DRESS, 1914

1–3. Privates, marching order — 4. Private, battle order — Regimental badges:
5. Oxfordshire and Buckinghamshire Light Infantry — 6. Somerset Light Infantry — 7. Manchester Regiment (1923-pattern) — 8. The King's Regiment — 9. Northumberland Fusiliers — 10. Lancashire Fusiliers — 11. South Wales Borderers — 12. Royal Inniskilling Fusiliers — 13. Royal Welsh Fusiliers — 14. Gloucestershire Regiment — 15. The King's Royal Rifle Corps — 16. East Lancashire Regiment — 17. North Staffordshire Regiment — 18. The Buffs

5

6

7

8

9

1

18 THE BUFFS

2

3

4

10 LANCASHIRE THE FUSILIERS

11

12 INNISKILLING

13 ROYAL WELSH FUSILIERS

14 EGYPT GLOUCESTERSHIRE

15

16 EGYPT LANCASHIRE

17 NORTH STAFFORD

The Helmet

In 1915, the troops in the front line were issued with steel helmets, the silhouette of which is familiar to all. This helmet soon became a general issue to both the British Army and the Armies of the Dominions and Colonies. It was painted in various colours ranging from light khaki to olive and from light grey to blue-grey (Tank Corps). Following the fashion of the Allies, the helmet was sometimes covered with coarse cloth on which was painted the regimental badge, occasionally it was camouflaged. As the British steel helmet had no crest and was made of a single piece of metal, it was far more easily manufactured than the French 'Adrian' helmet.

The Officers

The officers were easily recognizable by their Sam Browne belts, a combination of a waist-belt and a shoulder-belt, with the pistol-holster containing a Webley pistol and the ammunition pouch. The French and Belgian officers with their out-of-date uniforms envied the smart, neat and practical appearance of the British officers.

After their first encounter with the enemy, the British officers put aside their now useless swords and took to carrying sticks. Likewise, the brass buttons and the too-visible badges of rank on the cuffs fell into disfavour and the rank was shown on the shoulder-straps instead. So that they should be less conspicuous, the officers often carried rifles when going into the attack.

According to rank and appointment, either drab riding breeches and leggings or khaki pantaloons and puttees were worn. In Rifle Regiments, the buttons were black. The Foot Guards wore rather narrow plus-fours instead of pantaloons.

THE SCOTTISH REGIMENTS

The arrival of the first Highland Regiments caused great excitement on the Continent. The strange, skirted soldiers nevertheless acquitted themselves well in the struggle and subsequent retreat of the first few weeks. In appearance, they had little in common with the rest of the British Infantry, apart from their arms and equipment. For the most part, the Scots Regiments wore the glengarry.

The Black Watch wore a plain blue glengarry with a small red *tourie* (little pom-pom), The Argyll and Sutherland Highlanders wore a red and white diced band, The Cameronians had a rifle green glengarry with a black *tourie* and the other Regiments, both Highland and Lowland, wore a blue glengarry with a red, white and dark green diced band. The Scots Guards, apart from the pipers, dressed as Foot Guards but their blue forage caps had red, white and green diced bands and were without chinstraps; on some other head-dresses, they had a patch of the same design as the dicing at the side. In some Regiments, a khaki tam-o'-shanter was worn.

The jacket differed from that worn by other regiments in that it had the fronts rounded off at the skirt. The coloured hose and white spats were replaced by khaki stockings and matching gaiters or puttees.

BRITISH INFANTRY, 1914–18

1. Officer (1914) — 2–3. Lewis light machine gun team — 4. Bomber — 5. Corporal, in a light infantry regiment — 6. Machine-gunner (1914) and Vickers machine gun with tripod and condenser — 7. Winter dress, of which there were many varieties — 8. Modified equipment for No 1 on Vickers and Lewis guns — 9. Right-hand cartridge carrier, 1908 web equipment — 10. Mark III rifle and bayonet — 11. Lewis light machine gun — 12. Webley pistol, Mark V (twice the scale of the other weapons) — 13. Bayonet and scabbard, with entrenching-tool handle attached

The Kilt

The kilt, which is a traditional part of Highland dress, is made of woollen material woven in variegated patterns that have, in some cases, become associated with particular clans. These patterns are known as tartans and are of considerable complexity.

In action, a khaki apron was worn over the kilt and this usually had a pocket in front in place of the sporran which, in fact, is an ornamented pouch.

Pipers

The pipers are part of the Scottish tradition and there were normally two pipers to each company. These men, with their bagpipes, played their comrades into action. Piper Laidlaw of The King's Own Scottish Borderers, who stood on the parapet and played his pipes as the men went over the top at Loos in 1915, will be remembered for all time.

The Officers

The officer's service dress jacket had the skirts rounded in front after the manner of the doublet. The broad sword, commonly called the claymore, like the swords of the other Infantry officers was quickly laid aside.

MACHINE-GUNS

In 1912, the British Army adopted the Vickers machine-gun, which soon proved itself one of the most effective weapons of its type. It had a rate of fire of 450 to 550 rounds per minute, and fired the standard British ·303 in ammunition. The feed-belts held 250 rounds. .

The Lewis gun, a light machine-gun, appeared in 1915 and was issued on a large scale to the infantry. It likewise fired the standard ammunition. The magazine held 47 rounds.

The gun numbers wore the normal infantry dress but the No. 1 on the gun, the man who actually fired it, was armed with a pistol instead of a rifle.

Gasmasks

The first type of gasmask, the M2, was carried in a bag, and the A.R.S. model in a metal tube. The use of poison gas in the Ypres Salient on 22 April 1915, as one might have expected, caused absolute panic but fortunately for the Allies, the Germans did not know how to turn this to their own advantage.

The gas used in the first instance, was a mixture of chlorine and nitrogen peroxide and this could poison the atmosphere to a depth of $1\frac{1}{4}$ miles. The discharge of the gas was a simple matter: one container of about 1 cwt of liquid chlorine could, by the simple expedient of opening a tap at the end of a tube some two yards long, release more than 40 gallons of gas per yard of front, thus contaminating a considerable area. Gas-shells were also used.

After the initial shock and when the gas had been analysed, a gas-mask, fitted with a window, that covered the nose, mouth and eyes was devised. In the air-intake, there was a wadding plug soaked in a 10% solution of sodium hyposulphite which absorbed the chlorine. Next, a small quantity of sodium carbonate was added to the solution to neutralise the hydrochloric acid that formed.

BRITISH INFANTRY:
SCOTTISH REGIMENTS, 1914

Officers: 1. Black Watch — 2. Cameron Highlanders — 3. Gordon Highlanders, Ensign with Regimental Colour — 4. Gordon Highlanders — 5. Highland Light Infantry

1   2   3   4   5

L.×F.FUNCKEN

In due course, the German chemists evolved other gases such as bromine, various nitrogen compounds, hydrogen sulphide and mustard gas, which also blistered the skin.

All sorts of devices were thought up to give protection against this diabolical weapon starting with an improved gas-mask, known as the 'pig's-snout' (*groin de cochon*), made in a single piece and copied from the Germans. All sorts of alarms, too, were used ranging from bells to motor-horns. Anti-gas powders were spread in the trenches and dug-outs and fires were lighted along the parapets of the trenches to try and drive the clouds of deadly gas upwards. Another method was to let off gunpowder charges in front of the gas clouds in order to break them up. Nevertheless, countless unfortunate men were gassed and spent the remainder of their days as incurable asthmatics.

THE INDIAN, DOMINION, AND COLONIAL FORCES

Loyal to the Crown, the countries of the Empire felt it an honour to come to the assistance of the British Army. Canada, India, Australia and New Zealand sent about a million men between them.

In Canada, enthusiastic volunteers collected in a huge camp on the outskirts of Quebec and, after a short period of training, embarked for Great Britain on 3 October 1914. More hurriedly, a second draft was despatched direct to France in February 1915. At first they were placed under the British command but, at the end of 1916, the Canadians who by then had four divisions, were formed into the Canadian Army Corps under the Canadian General, Sir Arthur Currie. 600,000 Canadian volunteers came forward in all.

Canada also provided a considerable quantity of supplies and ammunition which, in the process, brought her important industrial expansion. After the war, Canada was a separate signatory to the Peace Treaty. She had lost 60,000 men.

Australia and New Zealand found the Australian and New Zealand Army Corps (ANZAC), who fought with distinction in France, Egypt and Palestine.

The Indian Army, including the Sikhs and the Gurkhas, upheld its fine traditions in the Flanders mud.

South Africa played an important part in the War, both fighting against the Germans in their colonies in South West Africa and sending a Brigade with ancillary troops to France.

Among the Canadian, Australian and South African troops, there were Regiments with Scottish traditions that, like their counterparts in Scotland, wore the kilt.

THE AUXILIARY FORCES

In addition to the Regular Army in 1914, into which large numbers of extra men were enlisted 'for the duration' and formed into the New Armies, there also existed the Special Reserve and the Territorial Force, both formed in 1908.

The Special Reserve was formed from the Militia which dated from the Restoration in 1660. On the outbreak of war, the Battalions of the Special Reserve functioned as training and reinforcement units.

BRITISH INFANTRY:
HIGHLANDERS, SERVICE DRESS

1–2. Officers (1914) — 3. Service dress (1916–18) — 4–5. Service dress (1914) — 6–7. Service dress (1915) — 8. Seaforth Highlanders, Glengarry badge — 9. Seaforth Highlanders, Collar badges

1

2

8

9

3

4

5

6

7

45

L. & F. FUNCKEN

The Territorial Force, which embraced all arms and services, was formed from the Yeomanry (volunteer cavalry) and the Volunteers (artillery, engineers, infantry and services). Originally, it was liable for service only in the United Kingdom, but its members were allowed to volunteer to serve elsewhere, which they all did when the time came.

The Territorials wore the same uniforms as the Regulars, but some units were still armed with the Long Lee-Enfield Rifle, which had been superseded in the Regular Army in 1907. This, however, was only a temporary measure. They had small Regular Cadres who were responsible for their discipline and training, both of which were of the highest standard.

THE BRITISH EXPEDITIONARY FORCE

There has been some criticism of the huge recruiting campaign launched by the British Government when Britain entered the War. Indeed it may have been unnecessary because men flocked to the Colours. The barrack accommodation available was insufficient, and camps were set up. When, in 1916, the new divisions landed in France, they soon made their presence felt as they took their place in the line beside the exhausted *poilus*. However, it was the Territorials formed the first reinforcements to the original British Expeditionary Force (BEF).

At Mons on the morning of 23 August 1914, the BEF was occupying a 15-mile front, with a gap of about 12 miles on the right between it and the French 5th Army. It was only just beginning to dig in when, at 10 o'clock in the morning, the Germans appeared. Although checked at first by the artillery, they continued to advance and it was then that they had their first taste of the British sustained rapid fire of the Lee-Enfield rifles. During the afternoon, the Germans renewed the attack, but no longer in close order, which reduced their casualties as compared with those sustained earlier in the day. To give an example, in one attack the 12th Brandenburg Grenadiers lost 25

BRITISH ARMY AND COLONIAL CONTINGENTS: IDENTIFICATIONS, 1914–18

Officers' Badges of Rank: 1. Second Lieutenant — 2. Lieutenant — 3. Captain — 4. Major — 5. Lieutenant-Colonel — 6. Colonel
The Badges of Rank worn on the shoulder-strap were common to all Arms of the Service: the cuff badges shown were worn by all Arms, except the Household Cavalry, the Brigade of Guards, the Scottish Regiments and Army Chaplains.
7. Brigadier-General — 8. Major General — 9. Lieutenant-General — 10. General — 11. Field Marshal
Other Ranks' Chevrons and Badges of Rank:
16. Regimental Sergeant-Major (up to 1915) then Company Sergeant-Major (the badge was worn on the lower arm, never above the elbow) — 17. Staff-Sergeant — 18. Sergeant and Lance-Sergeant — 19. Corporal — 20. Lance-Corporal (but not Foot Guards)
These are just a few of a very large number of Badges of Rank worn by the Other Ranks. They do not apply to the Household Cavalry nor, except broadly, to the Brigade of Guards.
Marksmanship and Tradesmen's Badges:
14. Pioneer — 15. Bomber — 22. Driver — 23. Best Shot in Company — 24. Machine-gunner — 25. Bandsman — 26. Scout
Shoulder titles:
27. Machine Gun Corps — 28–33. As shown
Decorations:
12. Distinguished Service Cross (a Naval decoration) — 13. Military Cross
Miscellaneous:
21. Overseas Service chevrons: Red, 1914; Blue, subsequent years.
Notes:
(a) The vertical stripes on 19 and 20 are Wound Stripes
(b) The blue triangle on 19 is a Divisional Sign
(c) The Crossed Rifles in 19 is a Marksman's badge
(d) The red disc with the numeral in 20 is the Battalion Numeral.

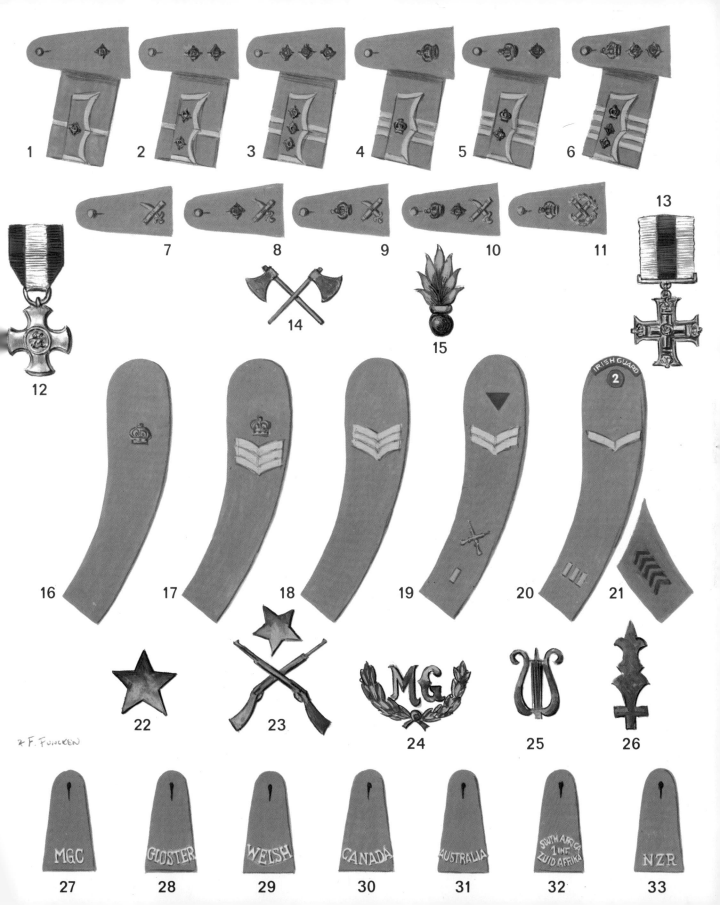

1
2
3
4
5
6
7
8
9
10
11
12
13
14
15
16
17
18
19
20
21
22
23
24
25
26
27 MGC
28 GLOSTER
29 WELSH
30 CANADA
31 AUSTRALIA
32 SOUTH AFRICA 1 INF. ZUID AFRIKA
33 NZR

IRISH GUARD
2

F. FUNCKEN

officers and 500 men from the fire of a Battalion of The Queen's Own Royal West Kent Regiment. Henceforth, the Germans revised their opinions of the British soldier, and many of their officers openly praised his courage.

Towards evening, the British started to fall back, for the French 5th Army was already in retreat and the BEF was in danger of being encircled by the Germans. However the withdrawal was carried out in an orderly manner to the amazement of the enemy, though not without severe losses. A battalion, engaged in a rearguard action at the village of Audregnies, fought to the last man and the last round. Nor were military traditions forgotten: to the consternation of the locals who held it to be downright sacrilege, the men of The Royal Welch Fusiliers buried their regimental mascot, a goat, with full military honours in the village cemetery.

The retreat dragged on for fifteen days, with only short halts for sleep and little to eat. On the third day, at Le Cateau on 26 August, the British again gave battle and II Corps lost nearly 2,000 men. Then the French under Foch intervened and their 5th Army counterattacked, checking the German advance under von Bülow at the Battle of St Quentin on 29 August 1914.

The Allied withdrawal continued and this was construed by the German generals, von Bülow and von Kluck, as a headlong flight. Wishing to turn the situation to their own advantage, von Kluck disregarded the orders of the High Command and turned the German 1st Army towards the south-east, thus exposing his left flank to the French 6th Army and to the divisions held in reserve in Paris. This allowed the French General Gallieni, along with the British, to launch an attack against the Germans and resulted in the victory of the Marne in September 1914.

A few days later, the German Commander-in-Chief, Helmuth von Moltke[25], was replaced by Erich von Falkenhayn[26].

There is a British military dictum: 'When you can advance no further, dig a hole and hold that.' That is precisely what happened: both sides dug themselves in using a complicated network of trenches.

From then on, the British Army found itself involved in a period of static warfare, compared with which the sieges of the past were of little account. The lessons of the fairly recent Russo-Japanese War were ignored by the strategists of Europe who, though realising their mistake, nevertheless clung to their pet theories, so inflicting on the troops a terrible disadvantage.

Even Lord Kitchener[27], still thinking in terms of the Transvaal no doubt, maintained that the British infantry had no need of artillery support to capture a position.

In Artois in September 1915, the combined French and British offensive resulted in 380,000 casualties of whom 120,000 were killed. On the Somme in 1916, the British lost 400,000 in five months, 60,000 of them fell in the first two days. These terrific losses were due to the excessive confidence that was placed in the preliminary artillery bombardment which was designed to drive the enemy underground.

In March 1918, the Germans launched an

25 Helmuth von Moltke (1848–1916) was the nephew of the more famous Marshal who conducted operations in the Prussian War of 1866 and the Franco-Prussian War of 1870–1. He was also known as a painter and poet, he played the violin.
26 Erich von Falkenhayn (1861–1922) later commanded the German troops in Palestine later in the War.
27 Field Marshal Earl Kitchener of Khartoum (1850–1916) had a most distinguished career in the British Army and was made Secretary of State for War in 1914. It was due to him that Britain managed to put her vast armies into the field.

BRITISH INFANTRY, 1915–18

1–2. Black Watch (with the red 'tourie') — 3. Northumberland Fusiliers, with cap with ear-flaps — 4. Private (1917–18) — 5. Private with gas-mask — 6–7. Privates, battle order, winter dress: 6 with the first pattern gas-mask.

offensive with thirty-six divisions supported by 6,000 guns, and the British, outnumbered two to one, were compelled to bring up every possible man from the rear to provide reinforcements. The Germans attacked again, this time with thirty-eight divisions against eight, but the 3rd Army under General Byng, who had the happy idea of evacuating the first line and keeping the second line intact, halted the advance. A new defensive tactic was thus evolved and it was used on a large scale by Pétain. Indeed, after the arrival of the fifteen United States divisions, it was to break down the morale and the resistance of the Germans.

According to the estimates of the U.S. War Department, the British Empire lost 908,371 killed, and 2,090,212 wounded in the course of the War.

INDIAN AND COLONIAL INFANTRY

1. Gurkha Officer, Indian Army — 2. Sikh sepoy, Indian Army — 3. Australian soldier — 4. Canadian lance-corporal — 5. Punjabi Mussalman Subadar, Indian Army — 6. Punjabi Mussalman sepoy, Indian Army — 7. New Zealand — 8. Askari, East Africa

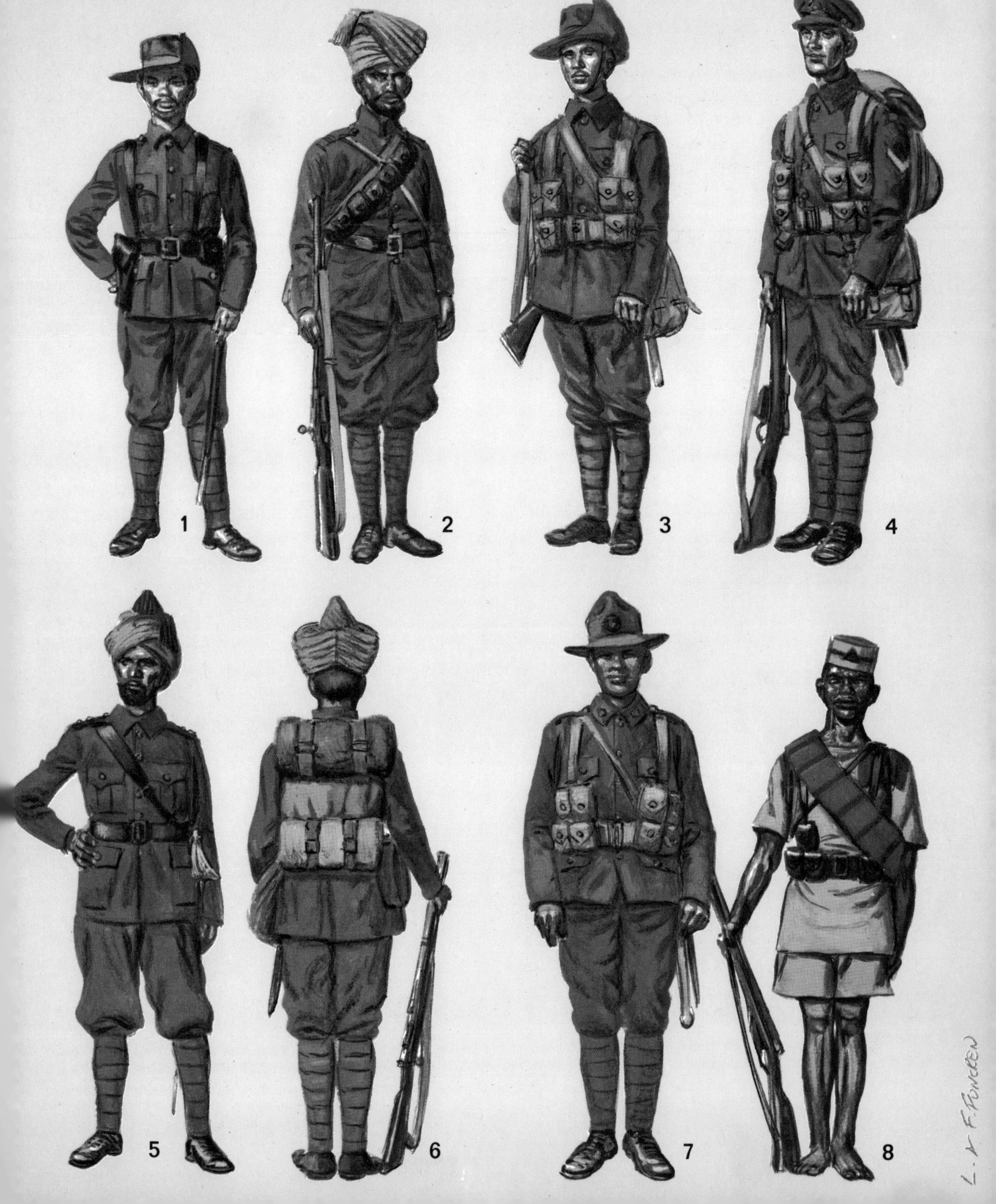
1
2
3
4
5
6
7
8

The Russian Infantry

Russia mobilised on 31 July 1914. There was a great show of patriotic fervour and determination to uphold the right to existence of the small state of Serbia; Austria-Hungary had just declared war upon her, blaming her for the murder of the Archduke Franz Ferdinand at Sarajevo.

Compulsory military service had been introduced by the Tzar Alexander II (1855–81) in 1861. The Russian Army was of a very considerable size and, in the rather mistaken ideas of the time, was truly a 'steam roller'.

Both in Russia and elsewhere, all that seemed to be remembered of the humiliating defeat suffered by Russia in the War against Japan in 1904–5 was the destruction of the Russian fleet. In the present instance however, the Russians would provide a second front and even the most pessimistic observers drew consolation from the thought of the hundreds of regiments that were on call. The Germans, on the other hand, had already formulated plans to deal with this eventuality.

THE INFANTRY

The Russian Infantry consisted of 353 regiments, of which sixteen were Grenadiers and twelve belonged to the Guards. Space does not permit of our listing the identifications of all these, so we shall content ourselves with giving only those of

Regiment	Collar	Cuffs	Cuff-patches	Lapels
Preobrajenski	red	red, with white piping		red
Semenov	bright blue, with red piping	red, with white piping		red
Ismaïlov	dark green, with red piping	red, with white piping		red
Chasseurs	dark green, with red piping	red, with white piping		light green with white piping
Moscow		all red		
Pavlov Grenadiers	bright blue, with red piping		all red	
Pavlov	dark green, with red piping		all red	
Finland	dark green, with red piping	red		dark green
Lithuania	yellow, with dark green piping		all yellow	
Kexholm Grenadiers	bright blue, with yellow piping		all yellow	
St Petersburg Grenadiers	dark green, with yellow piping		all yellow	
Volhynia	dark green, with yellow piping	yellow	dark green	

RUSSIAN INFANTRY: PARADE DRESS I

1. Ensign, with Colour, 2nd Sofiiski Regiment — 2. General Officer, 84th Chirvanski Regiment — 3. Corporal, 34th Sevski Regiment — 4. Bugler, 51st Litovski Regiment — 5. Drummer, 9th Inkermanlandski Regiment — 6. Private, 13th Erivanski Grenadiers — 7. Warrant Officer, 6th Tavritcheski Grenadiers — 8. Corporal, 8th Apcheronski Regiment

6

7

2

8

3 4

1

5

L. & F. Funcken

the twelve Regiments of the Guard as they were in 1914.

In all cases, the uniform was dark green. The first eight Regiments had red trouser stripes and brass buttons. In all cases, the loops on the collar, cuffs and cuff-patches were yellow. In full dress, the Pavlov Grenadiers wore the old mitre-cap.

As the illustrations show, the peace-time uniform was very like that worn during the Napoleonic Wars, the parade dress with the plumed shako was particularly so, though the plumes were removed in drill order. A number of orders of dress were worn. Besides the foregoing, there were service dress, working dress and summer dress. This last consisted of a blouse worn outside the breeches.

The catastrophes of the Russo-Japanese War led to the adoption of another order of dress, campaign dress, which was grey-green and better suited to modern warfare. In winter, a fur cap replaced the service dress cap which resembled the German cap in shape, a sheep-skin cape was worn with this.

The infantry of the line wore their regimental numerals in yellow on the shoulder-straps, the light infantry in red. The great-coat, which was slightly greener than the rest of the uniform, and the rest of the equipment had been retained after the previous war. The men were called up at the age of twenty-one and had to serve for three and a half years with the colours, followed by a reserve liability for fourteen and a half years. He was then transferred to the militia for a further four years.

The Russian army on a war footing comprised three categories: the active army, the reserves and the supply and maintenance organisation, with a total strength of 4,100,000 combatant troops.

The Russian Army was organised in the usual way in divisions, brigades and regiments. Thus the 1st Division consisted of the 1st and 2nd Brigades, composed respectively of the 1st and 2nd Regiments and the 3rd and 4th Regiments. This system carried on which made it very simple for a spy to build up the Russian Order of Battle.

The Rifle

The Russian infantry was armed with the Mosin-Nagant rifle, adopted in 1891. The magazine had been improved by a Belgian, named Nagant, and the charger held five ·3 in rounds. The rifle weighed $9\frac{1}{4}$ lb and was 4 ft 3 in long. It could be fired single-shot or repeating and had a muzzle velocity of only 2034 feet per second, which gave an effective range of somewhat over 500 yards, compared with the French Lebel rifle that had an effective range of nearly 740 yards. The bayonet, which was tapered, was about 20 in in length, and was always carried fixed on service.

The Equipment

Basically, the equipment was a large wallet which was carried on the left and contained 60 rounds of reserve ammunition, the man's necessaries, a mug, three pairs of socks and a change of underclothes. A proper valise was only carried by the Guards. In line regiments, it was replaced by a plain bag closed by a running cord.

The most obvious feature of the Russian uniform was the greatcoat which was carried, rolled in a cover, with the ends inserted in the mess-tin on the right hip. The mess-tin, which had no lid, was of aluminium with a galvanised iron wire handle. The water-bottle, also of aluminium, had a cloth cover. The ammunition pouches, which were of an out-of-date type, were of yellow leather and held 30 rounds each.

Each company had 80 shovels and 20 axes, and there was one tent for every six men. On service, the man carried reserve rations consisting of biscuits, salt, tea and sugar for three days, together with dried meat for one day.

RUSSIAN INFANTRY: PARADE DRESS II

1. General of Infantry — 2. Private, Life Guard Regiment Pavlov (the last to retain the mitre-cap) — 3. Field Officer, Life Guard Regiment Preobraschenski — 4. Private, Life Guard Grenadier Regiment — 5. Sergeant, Finlandski Regiment — 6. Bandsman, Litovski Regiment — 7. General of Infantry

2   3   4   5

1   6   7

L. & F. FUNCKEN

THE OFFENSIVE THAT ENDED IN DISASTER

Although it appeared formidable, the Russian Army had many shortcomings. In the first place, mobilisation took a full month, because huge areas of the country had only a rudimentary rail network.

The Russian soldier was possessed of a stoical courage, not unmixed with fatalism born of centuries of serfdom, but this was of little avail when he had to go into battle unarmed until one of his comrades fell and he could take his rifle. Such was the supply shortage that, in some units, there was only one rifle between six men. Many of the officers were incompetent but in any case they too were ill-equipped; if they had compasses they had no maps; and this made the men easy targets for subversive activities. Thus, it was not long before they rose in revolt against a *régime* that only got worse. However that may be, following the maxim of the Czar Alexander I, the Russian army went into the attack 'sword in hand and true to the faith'.

The first encounter was at Gumbinnen on 18 August 1914, where the Germans under von Prittwitz were driven back by Rennenkampf after fierce fighting. The demoralised German 8th Army fell back, taking advantage of the fact that the Russian commander had allowed his exhausted troops to rest for a day after eight days of forced marches.

After a moment's panic when he feared he might lose his throne, the German Emperor saved the situation by calling back from retirement the sixty-seven-year-old General von Hindenburg to replace the unhappy Prittwitz. Hindenburg took the matter in hand with the calm and energy that were characteristic of him, ably assisted by Ludendorff, and decided to concentrate his efforts on the Russian 2nd Army under Samsonov, who was advancing in the south with the intention of taking the German 8th Army from behind.

After his initial victory, for reasons best known to himself, Rennenkampf stayed where he was. This gave the Germans the opportunity they needed and, from 23 August, they brought pressure to bear on the Russian 2nd Army, which was separated from the Russian 1st Army by over 90 miles. To the delight of the Germans, the two Russian Armies communicated with each other by wireless, in clear (i.e. not in code).

On 26 August 1914, the German 8th Army fell upon Samsonov and, in three days, surrounded his forces. The Russians tried to break out but were forced back everywhere by the intense fire of the Germans. Finally, on the evening of 30 August, they surrendered and Samsonov committed suicide. The Germans took 90,000 prisoners. This victory, which the Germans named Tannenberg[28], had less effect strategically than is generally supposed for the Russian Army was far from having been destroyed. Its effect on morale, on the other hand, was enormous for it bolstered up the notion of the invincibility of the German Army.

Without delay, Hindenburg turned north against Rennenkampf who, inexplicably, had still done nothing. On 7 September, the Germans attempted to force the passage of the Masurian Lakes but, fighting stubbornly, the Russians con-

---

28 In 1410, the Teutonic Knights had been defeated at a battle of that name. The glory of this new victory removed the shame of the original defeat.

RUSSIAN IDENTIFICATIONS

1. Marshal — 2. General — 3. Lieutenant-General — 4. Major-General — 5. Colonel — 6. Lieutenant-Colonel (Major, with two stars) — 7. Captain — 8. Second Captain — 9. Lieutenant — 10. Second Lieutenant — 11. Probationary Second Lieutenant — 12. Warrant Officer, 1st Class — 13. Warrant Officer, 2nd Class — 14. Staff Sergeant — 15. Sergeant — 16. Corporal — 17. Private — 18. Private, service dress — 19. 1st, 2nd, 3rd and 4th Guards Infantry — 20. Grenadiers — 21–22. Infantry of the Line — 23. *Tirailleurs* — 24. Guards Infantry — 25. Marker, Siberian Infantry — 26. Telegraphist — 27. Machine-gunner — 28. Wireless operator — 29. Cyclist

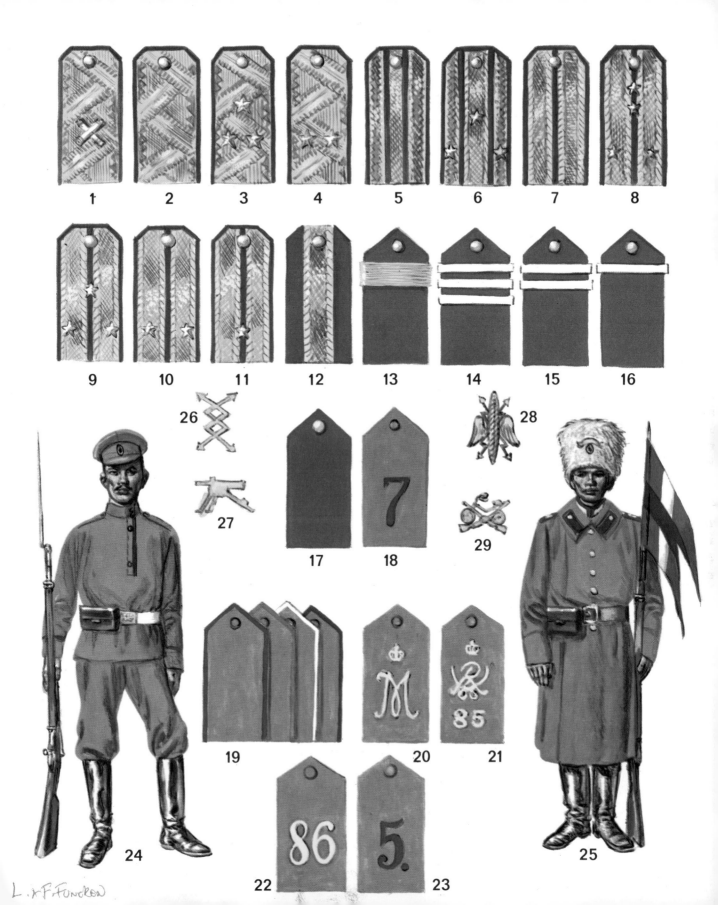

L. & F. Funcken

tained the assault and Rennenkampf, making full use of his reserves, avoided being surrounded and fell back on the River Niemen which he crossed during 13–15 September.

Thus, the Russian offensive against the Germans ended with the Russians worse off than when they started. On the Austrian front, however, the Russians were able to draw some consolation in their military misfortunes. Wishing to help their German allies who were in difficulties in East Prussia before Hindenburg's arrival on the scene, the Austrians had, on 21 August, launched a hasty and ill-prepared offensive against inferior numbers of Russian forces in Galicia. In an initial victory, they had taken tens of thousands of prisoners and had invaded Russian soil. On 2 September 1914, the Russians under the general-issimo, the Grand Duke Nicholas, an uncle of the Czar, counter-attacked strongly driving the Austro-Hungarian armies back all along the line and compelling them to abandon 120,000 prisoners and several hundred guns. The deterioration of the situation forced the Germans to pull out considerable forces from the Western Front hurriedly. Although this enabled them to hold the Eastern Front, it weakened their position at the Battle of the Marne.

The German plans for France having broken down on the Marne, the Central Powers decided to launch a series of offensives against the Russians, spread over a very wide front. Fifty-nine German divisions and fifty Austro-Hungarian divisions were assembled for the purpose and simultaneous attacks were made from East Prussia in the north-east, to Galicia in the south-east, starting on 26 September. At first, the Russian line held. How-ever, on 28 September, the Grand Duke Nicholas only just managed to hold Hindenburg's main thrust towards Warsaw. In the south, the Austrians managed to break through on 4 October but a few days later the Russians retook the ground and captured 120,000 prisoners. In the centre, a counter-attack drove Hindenburg back and the very frontier of Germany seemed threatened.

The situation was critical, and not only for Austria. The German High Command decided that the matter must be settled and they launched what, according to witnesses, was one of the bloodiest offensives of the war. Germany was convinced that it was absolutely essential to eliminate the Russian menace; then, she would have her hands free to deal with the Western Front. The Russian armies were driven back but, although they lost 3,800,000 killed, wounded and taken prisoner, they still constituted a threat in the east.

The Russians had been driven back nearly 170 miles and this serious reverse was to have far-reaching consequences. At the instance of the Tzarina, the Tzar replaced his uncle as general-issimo and put himself at the head of his Army. His experience as a soldier was limited to drilling a battalion of the Preobrajenski Regiment, of which he was Colonel. Fortunately, however, he did not presume to conduct operations himself but en-trusted this to an excellent officer, General Alexeïev.

The removal of the Grand Duke Nicholas, who was very popular and was much respected by the Army in particular, proved catastrophic. There are many stories about him, born no doubt of his forceful character, for this national hero had never been in the front line as he was terrified of stray bullets. His disappearance from the scene coin-cided with the moment when, after a retreat that resembled all too closely the retreat of 1812 complete with a 'scorched earth' policy, the Russian Army was totally demoralised. The

RUSSIAN INFANTRY: SERVICE DRESS I

1. Officer — 2. Foot soldier, in winter service dress with sheepskin hat — 3–4. Guards Infantry — 5. Officer, wearing comforter — 6. Infantry of the Line — 7. Guards Infantry — 8. Infantry of the Line — 9. Order of St. George, 4th Class — 10. Order of St Stanislaus, with Swords, 3rd Class — 11. Order of St Vladimir, Civil Division, 4th Class — 12. Haversack, Infantry of the Line — 13. Haversack, Guards — 14. Water-bottle — 15. Individual cooking pot

clumsy attempts on the part of the Tzar to gain the affection of the men were repulsed.

The Central Powers thought that, by now, the Russian Army was definitely despondent but, notwithstanding their misfortunes, the Russians made a sudden recovery and, urged on by General Broussilov, returned to the attack on 4 June 1916. The Austro-Hungarian Army in Galicia collapsed leaving 150,000 prisoners in Russian hands[29]. In two months, Broussilov had taken 400,000 prisoners, of whom 80,000 were Germans, and he had recovered a considerable amount of territory but, when the Germans counter-attacked with twenty-three hastily assembled divisions, the Russians were once more driven back, this time decisively.

The Russian front had ceased to exist, and, after the abdication of the Tzar in March 1917, the new *régime* was unable to restore order in the Army. A few months later, the October Revolution enabled Lenin to seize power, and he at once sued for peace. He secured an armistice, ordered general demobilisation and, on 3 March 1918, signed the Peace Treaty of Brest-Litovsk with the Central Powers.

29 The military operations in the Caucasus will be dealt with in the section on the Turkish army.

RUSSIAN INFANTRY: SERVICE DRESS II

1. Guards Infantry (as on the Vistula, 1914) — 2. Infantry of the Line — 3. Ensign, with cased Colour — 4. Infantry of the Line — 5. Private, Infantry of the Line, with French 'Adrian' steel helmet bearing badge of the Russian Imperial Arms (as on the Macedonian Front)

The Italian Infantry

Italy, after much hesitation, decided to enter the War on the side of the Allies in August 1915. It must be remembered that, at this time, Italy was a party to the Triple Alliance[30], which bound her to Germany and Austria-Hungary. When she decided to remain neutral, at least for the time being, Italy was in fact offering herself to the highest bidder whether it might be the Central Powers or the Allies, both of whom wanted to gain her military support in return for substantial territorial aggrandisements. As these aggrandisements would be, for the most part, at the expense of Austria, the Allies won the bidding.

On paper, the Italian Army had an effective strength of 3,500,000 men, but all that the Italians could find to assist the Allies were 900,000 troops. The liability for compulsory military service started at the age of twenty: two years with the colours, six years in the regular reserve, four years with the militia and finally seven years with the territorials. The peace time army was 289,448 men strong.

In 1914, the infantry consisted of ninety-four Line regiments, two grenadier regiments, twelve regiments of *Bersaglieri* (rifles) and eight alpine regiments. By 1915, there were thirty-six divisions, comprising 560 battalions which included sixty-two alpine battalions and sixty-six battalions of *Bersaglieri*.

UNIFORM AND ARMS

The Italian Army wore a greenish-grey uniform which had been adopted for service dress in 1908. Each brigade consisted of two Line regiments, and had a distinctive collar patch, pointed at the lateral end. The *Bersaglieri* and the alpine battalions had flame-shaped collar patches. For all, there was a five-pointed white-metal star at the end of the collar patch.

The Helmet

The Italian helmet was of the French pattern but made in one piece at first. There are, however, numerous photographs that show helmets with a crest that has been attached separately. This helmet was painted the same colour as the uniform or sometimes in a slightly darker shade. The arm of service badge was stencilled on the front and was of the same design as the cap badge.

The Equipment

Basically, the equipment was a waterproof canvas valise, light and practical. There were several patterns, the standard pattern haversack was greenish in colour and was worn on the left hip. The water-bottle, which was covered with green-grey cloth, was worn on the right.

The Rifle

The Italian rifle was a Mannlicher-Carcano, 1891-pattern, ·246 in, with a six-round magazine. It was probably the worst rifle used by any of the belligerents and its calibre was not its only weakness.

The Machine-guns

The Italian Army had a variety of machine-guns, of which most were Colts but it also had Austrian

---

30 The Triple Alliance was formed between Germany, Austria and Russia after the Franco-Prussian War. The Tzar withdrew in 1882 and Italy joined in 1887. The Alliance had last been renewed in 1912 for a five year period.

ITALIAN INFANTRY: SERVICE DRESS

1. Lance-Sergeant — 2. Sergeant (1916) — 3. Specially trained soldier, *Bersaglieri* — 4. Special Duty Troops, service dress — 5. Second Lieutenant — 6. Corporal, field service marching order — 7. Private, field service marching order — 8. Lieutenant — 9. Captain — 10. Brigadier — 11. Lieutenant-Colonel

Schwarzlose 1907–12-pattern, a large number of French St-Étienne, some Italian Revelli and some German Maxim guns.

THE 'ARDITI'

The *Arditi* originated in raiding parties organised to fall upon enemy outposts. With the advent of trench warfare, these developed into what would today be called commandos. Officially, they were known as 'volunteer scouts' (*volontari esploratori*) but they were commonly known, in modern terminology, as suicide squads (*compagnie della morte*).

In 1916, men specially trained in the use of explosives and in day and night reconnaissance were given the rating of *militare ardito* (keen soldier). Then, in 1917, the *arditi* were re-organised under Major Giuseppe Alberto Bassi, into assault groups (*reparti d'assalto*) and were given a distinctive uniform. In action, these troops were armed with a dagger and carried a dozen grenades. Sometimes they also carried a carbine of a pattern dating from 1891.

The *arditi* distinguished themselves particularly on the Piave, where they earned the nickname of the 'Piave Alligators'. In one action, Captain Remo Pontecorvo Bacci's frogmen lost fifty men out of a total of eighty-two.

THE COURSE OF THE WAR

While the Italian Government shilly-shallied, the Austrian Government prepared itself, foreseeing that Italy would turn upon her, and manned her alpine frontier. When Italy entered the war, the Austrians pulled out troops from the Russian front and it was these experienced men that opposed the enthusiastic but untried Italian Army. Committed regardlessly in mountainous country, the valiant Italian infantry soon had to stop for breath, while they tended 180,000 wounded and buried 66,000 dead. The losses were enormous, the military advantage negligible, but the outcome was that henceforward the Italian Army was held in low esteem.

The Italians pulled themselves together to the extent of improving their positions along the River Isonzo. The situation remained unchanged throughout the winter, but the Italians had to use all their ingenuity to maintain their position in the face of an enemy that occupied high ground overlooking them and that was much easier to defend.

On 15 May 1916, the Austrians launched a powerful offensive, which they styled a punitive operation, for they had not forgiven Italy for changing sides at the last minute. The Italian front line was quickly overrun but the advance soon slowed down and then stopped because, providentially, the Russian offensive on the Eastern Front forced the Austrians to withdraw a part of their Army from Italy. Thus they had to give up all hope of following up their initial success. In the summer of 1916, the Italians seized the initiative but, after the victory of Gorizia, they settled down in the autumn to a period of static warfare.

A particularly harsh winter lowered the morale of the Italian troops and there were many desertions because they considered that they were being sacrificed in a hopeless war of attrition. Among

ITALIAN INFANTRY:
SPECIAL DUTY TROOPS AND SMALL ARMS

1. Types of Special Duty Troops — 2. Carbine, 1891-pattern, with bayonet that folds back — 3. Carbine, 1891-pattern TS (*truppi speciali*), used by Special Duty Troops and *carabiniers* — 4. Rifle, 1891-pattern, Infantry of the Line — 5. Glisenti pistol, 1889-pattern, 10·35 mm — 6. Glisenti pistol, 1889-pattern, (without trigger-guard) with folding trigger. — 7. Brixia pistol, 1906-pattern, 9 mm — 8. Glisenti pistol, 1910-pattern, 9 mm — 9. Beretta pistol, 1915-pattern, 9 mm — 10. Beretta pistol, 1915-pattern, 7·65 mm — 11. Beretta pistol, 1915–19-pattern, 7·65 mm

ITALIAN INFANTRY: SERVICE DRESS

1. Lieutenant-Colonel, *Bersaglieri* (1916) — 2. Private, *Bersaglieri* — 3. Machine-gunners, *Bersaglieri*, with Revelli (Fiat) machine gun, 1914-pattern, 6·5 mm — 4. Colt machine gun, 1914-pattern, 6·5 mm — 5. Alpine Troops (1917)

5

them was a corporal of *Bersaglieri* who had been seriously wounded in February and in whose head ideas were being hatched that would have the most far-reaching consequences. His name was Benito Mussolini.

The collapse of Russia in October 1917 enabled the Germans to send some of their finest divisions to the assistance of the Austrians. On 24 October 1917, after a heavy barrage which included gas-shells, the German and Austrian overran the stunned enemy. Flame-throwers were used to clear up pockets of resistance and the attack was pushed right through to Caporetto. The Italian 2nd Army collapsed and fled and the German and Austrian forces broke through the gap. Taking advantage of the chaotic situation, they occupied the whole of the north-east of the Italian Peninsula in a fortnight, taking 300,000 prisoners and tens of thousands of guns and machine-guns[31]. The general opinion of the Italian Army sunk still lower after this catastrophe.

However, the Italians did not give up and they managed to hold on to the line of the River Piave, which runs through Venetia and flows into the Adriatic a few miles north of Venice. This natural barrier, which is nearly 140 miles·long, was attacked by the enemy but without artillery support and the attack failed.

Meanwhile 120,000 British and French troops were hurriedly despatched as reinforcements to the Piave. For seven days, the Italians, trying to recover their self-respect, held out successfully against the Germans and Austrians who were determined to cross the river. The attacks lasted from 20 to 27 November, when there was a respite. On 4 December, the enemy renewed their onslaught but the British and French reinforcements had arrived by then, and their presence at the battle galvanised the Italians to unprecedented acts of heroism.

After a long period of raid and counter-raid, the Austrians, no longer reinforced by the Germans who had been forced to move their troops to France, made another attempt to cross the Piave between 13 and 23 June 1918. The Italians made a strong counter-attack and drove the Austrians back from the Piave. The Austro-Hungarian Army, weakened by an epidemic of spanish influenza, gradually started to disintegrate and a mutiny of some of the Hungarian divisions on 20 October dealt the death blow.

31 The Italian defeat was blamed on the 'fact' that their army had no gas-masks. Actually they had an ample supply of French ones.

ITALIAN INFANTRY:
IDENTIFICATIONS AND HEAD-DRESSES
Distinctive collar patches for Brigades (two regiments in each)

Brigade–Regiments		Brigade–Regiments	
The King's	1–2	Piedmont	3–4
Aosta	5–6	Cuneo	7–8
The Queen's	9–10	Casale	11–12
Sinerola	13–14	Savona	15–16
Acqui	17–18	Brescia	19–20
Cremona	21–22	Como	23–24
Bergamo	25–26	Pavia	27–28
Pisa	29–30	Siena	31–32
Livorno	33–34	Pistoia	35–36
Ravenna	37–38	Bologna	39–40
Modena	41–42	Forli	43–44
Reggio	45–46	Ferrara	47–48
Parma	49–50	Alpi	51–52
Umbria	53–54	Marche	55–56
Abruzzi	57–58	Calabria	59–60
Sicily	61–62	Cagliari	63–64
Valtelina	65–66	Palermo	67–68
Ancona	69–70	Puglia	71–72
Lombardy	73–74	Naples	75–76
Tuscany	77–78	Rome	79–80
Turin	81–82	Venice	83–84
Verona	85–86	Friuli	87–88
Salerno	89–90		

Types of collar-patch:
1. Infantry of the Line — 2. Alpine Troops — 3. *Bersaglieri* — 4. Special Duty Troops
Head-dress badges:
5. Alpine Troops, on cap — 6. Infantry of the Line, on cap — 7. Infantry of the Line, on steel helmet — 9. *Bersaglieri*, on cap — 10. *Bersaglieri*, on distinctive head-dress (see Fig. 17) — 16. Special Duty Troops
Types of head-dress:
11. Steel helmet, Grenadiers — 12, 14. Steel helmet, Infantry of the Line — 13. Hat, Alpine Troops: 1st Battalion, white pom-pom; 2nd Battalion, red pom-pom; 3rd Battalion, green pom-pom; 4th Battalion, blue pom-pom; Depot Battalion, yellow pom-pom — 15. Cap, Infantry of the Line — 17. Hat, *Bersaglieri*
Miscellaneous:
8. Medal for Valour, 2nd Class — 18. Arm badge (left), Special Duty Troops

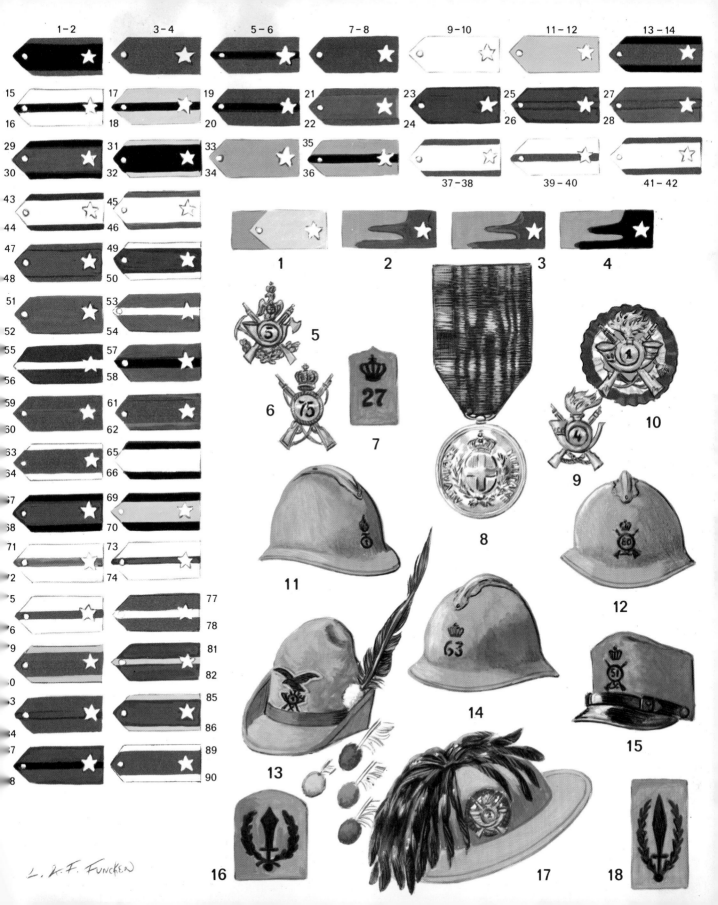

The Italians, with fifty-one divisions, supported by five British and French divisions and a division of Czecho-Slovak volunteers, attacked and broke the Austro-Hungarian resistance after three days of intense fighting. As the offensive built up, the enemy fell back all along the line. On 3 November 1918, the armistice was signed and the disgrace of Caporetto was avenged.

As is well-known, reproaches come more easily than praise and the Allies were luke-warm in their attitude to Italy's undoubted victory. When the day of reckoning came, Italy found herself cold-shouldered by her brothers-in-arms and their promises suddenly forgotten. With 650,000 killed, the country ruined and her hopes disappointed, Italy was easy prey for fascism. Twenty years later, she embarked upon an even more tragic venture and gave France, that ungrateful latin sister, the infamous stab in the back.

The American Expeditionary Force

After holding out against American public opinion which demanded an effective reply to Germany's provocations, President Woodrow Wilson realised at last the futility of his attempts to persuade the belligerents to accept the suggestions that, according to himself, would restore peace in Europe. The sinking of the Lusitania, on 7 May 1915, had already aroused the indignation of the American people and the continued attacks by German submarines from 1917 onwards tipped the scales. The Germans maintained that they had the right to stop all maritime traffic, in defiance of international law.

On 6 April 1917, the United States of America declared war on Germany, despite the protests of the champions of non-intervention, most of whom were recently naturalised Germans. In 1914, one in ten of the total population of the U.S.A. was German and they used such 'patriotic' bodies as the Organisation of American Women for Strict Neutrality as cover for their pro-German sympathies. This society, in 1915 opposed the supply of arms and ammunition to the Allies. These same organisations, at this time, were doing what they could to prevent the United States from building up its armed forces by invoking the Monroe Doctrine which dated from 1823 and preached American Non-Intervention outside the New World.

The result of these pro-German machinations was that, when America entered the war, she had only a skeleton army of 202,000 men and a corps of officers of less than 1,000.

The disembarkation of the first American troops in France, on 26 June 1917, was merely a token force. Indeed, since 17 May when the Senate had passed a law authorising the raising of contingents for service in Europe, there had been no waiting for volunteers to come forward. By the end of 1917, there were 1,225,000 American citizens in uniform and the figure had risen to 3,000,000 by November 1918.

The American Expeditionary Force (AEF) was placed under the command of Major-General John J. Pershing, an outstanding officer and a brilliant organiser who understood men and who

UNITED STATES OF AMERICA:
INFANTRY AND EQUIPMENT

1–2. Foot soldiers (in the service dress worn when they arrived in France in 1917) with Springfield rifles, 1903-pattern — 3. Valise and braces — 4. Valise, opened-up — 5–7. Waistbelt with cartridge-carriers, field-dressing pocket and wire-cutters and carrier — 8. Entrenching-tool — 9–10. Officers' collar-badges: the same designs were worn in relief on buttons on the collar by the enlisted men — 11. Knife, fork, spoon, plate and cooking-pan — 12–13. Water-bottles — 14. Mug

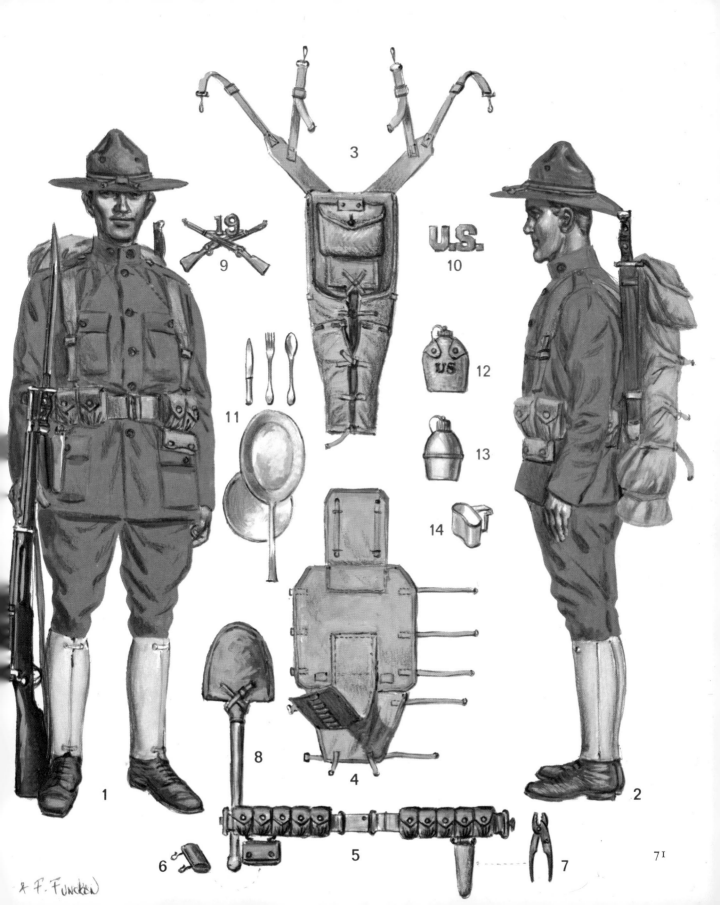

9

19

10

U.S.

11

12

US

13

14

3

8

4

1

2

5

6

7

71

A.F. Funcken

was descended from an Alsatian family that had settled in Baltimore in 1749. The officers who formed the backbone of this newly-fledged army had the advantage of belonging to something newly-formed, and they attended a three months' course in tactics on arrival in France.

The U.S. Army was organised in divisions, each of two brigades of two regiments. Each company was 250 strong. By the Armistice, the U.S.A. had sent forty-three such divisions to France, each 27,000 strong, almost four times that of some French divisions in 1917.

OFFICERS AND MEN

The first contingents of the AEF wore the standard khaki woollen uniform that had been in use since the beginning of the century. With the material made in a variety of different places in order to cope with the large influx of recruits, it appeared in a variety of colours ranging from brown to olive. The canvas leggings quickly disappeared because of the difficulties of making them, and were replaced by putties of the type worn in the British Army. For the same reason, the broad-brimmed hat gave place to a fore-and-aft cap and a steel helmet of the British pattern was taken into use.

The Equipment

The equipment was of a novel design and consisted, as may be seen from the illustration, of a wrapper which could be entirely opened out with a small detachable wallet at the top. It was light, well-constructed and did not encumber the wearer.

The Rifle

The American Springfield 1903-pattern, which was derived from a Spanish version of the German Mauser, was considered one of the best rifles in the world. The U.S. Government had acquired the rights of manufacture from the Germans for $200,000. It fired a ·3 in Spitzer bullet. Another rifle, the U.S. ·30 1917-pattern, was also in use; this was a modified version of the British Enfield rifle and was also known as a Springfield 1917.

The Light Machine-gun

The American Army had no weapons of this type so it adopted the French Cauchat light machine-gun, a weapon which had been developed by Chauchat, Sutter and Ribeyrolle at Puteaux. It fired a ·315 in Lebel bullet, and the semi-lunar magazine held twenty rounds. The American soldiers christened the weapon a 'shosho'.

The Badges

The other ranks wore a button on each side of the collar, that on the right side bore the letters 'U.S.' and that on the left showed the arm of service device and the regimental numeral. Other unofficial devices soon appeared at the top of the left arm of the jacket. The first of these was produced by the men of the 85th Division at the time of their embarkation for Europe in June 1918. Some of the officers objected to this, but the War Department thought it an excellent idea. Numerous other devices soon appeared and, in due course, they received the official designation of shoulder sleeve insignia.

Good Shooting Badges

The Good Shooting Badges, which were made of metal and were worn on the breast like medal ribbons, could only be gained after an intensive course with practices at 300 yards, 500 yards and 600 yards. The qualification of Marksman re-

UNITED STATES OF AMERICA:
SERVICE DRESS

1. Machine-gunner, with French Chauchat machine gun (1918) — 2. Officer, in great-coat with hood at back — 3. Non-commissioned officer, with regimental colour — 4. Battle order (summer 1918) with Springfield rifle, 1917-pattern, and gas-mask in haversack on chest — 5. Foot soldier (1918) the bayonet carried beside the valise.

quired 60% shots on the target, that of Sharp-shooter 75% and that of Expert Rifleman 90%, that is, 315 out of a possible of 350. Although these badges may appear rather ostentations and childish, they served to encourage marksmanship.

•

The Officers

Apart from the Sam Browne belt, copied from the British Army, and leather boots of various patterns, the officers of the AEF were dressed in the same way as the men, except that their badges of rank were worn on the shoulder.

The Americans have an amusing explanation of the origin of their badges of commissioned rank. As these badges were during the Great War, the Second-Lieutenant wore no badge as he was at the bottom of the ladder; the Lieutenant had a single silver bar as he was on the first rung of the ladder; the Captain had two bars; the Major, who had climbed some way into the tree, had a gilt maple leaf as he was still rather in the shade; the Lieutenant-Colonel had come out into the light so his maple leaf was silver; the Colonel was out of the wood and among the birds, so he wore an eagle; and the General Officers, who had really made the grade, were up in the stars, a Brigadier-General being distinguished by one, a Major-General by two, a Lieutenant-General by three and a General by four stars. Though probably not historically accurate, this acts as an excellent mnemonic.

The Colours

Every regiment carried two colours; a national colour, i.e. the Stars and Stripes, and a regimental colour. These were made of silk, and were both the same size.

THE COURSE OF THE WAR

The AEF were welcomed enthusiastically upon their arrival in France and, at first, were known as 'amex'. This, however, was soon changed to 'Sammies'[32]. They were provided with French instructors, mostly from the *Chasseurs*, who had battle experience, and the new-comers soon found themselves at one with the veterans.

The first casualties were incurred by the American 16th Infantry at Lunéville on 3 November 1917. Serving alongside French units at Craonne in March 1918, the Americans quickly learned how to face up to a ruthless enemy. In June and July 1918 during the offensive in the Champagne, twenty-seven U.S. divisions advanced side by side with the French to retake Château-Thierry. Then, in September, came St-Mihiel where 16,000 prisoners and 443 guns were taken. In October, the American Army took Varennes, Vauquois and Beaumont, then cleaned up the Forest of Argonne where, on 18 October 1918, Corporal Alvin C. York and his

---

32 'Amex' is an acronym derived from American Expeditionary Force. 'Sammy' is derived from 'Uncle Sam', the American counterpart of 'John Bull'.

UNITED STATES OF AMERICA:
IDENTIFICATIONS AND DECORATIONS

Badges of rank:
1. First Lieutenant (a Second Lieutenant had no badge) — 2. Captain — 3. Major — 4. Lieutenant-Colonel — 5. Colonel — 6. Brigadier-General — 7. Major-General — 8. Lieutenant-General (a General wore, at his own choice, either four stars or the Arms of the U.S.A. between two stars) — 9. Corporal (a Lance-Corporal had a single chevron) — 10. Sergeant — 11. First Sergeant — 12. Company Quartermaster-Sergeant — 13. Supply Sergeant — 14. Battalion Sergeant-Major — 15. Regimental Sergeant-Major — 16. Assistant Band Leader — 17. Sergeant-Bugler — 18. Band Leader — 19. Colour-Sergeant — 20. Drum-Major — 21. Battalion Quartermaster-Sergeant — 22. Regimental Quartermaster-Sergeant
Formation signs:
23. 85th Division (original device) — 24. 30th Division — 25. 40th Division — 26. 2nd Division — 27. Paris Division — 28. 371st Regiment (The Bloody Hand: Verdun) — 29. 93rd Division — 30. Commissariat — 31. 9th Corps — 32. 89th Division — 33. 94th Squadron, U.S. Air Force ('Hat in the Ring'), breast badge — 34. 27th Division
Decorations:
35. Distinguished Service Medal — 36. Congressional Medal of Honor — 37. Distinguished Service Cross
Marksmanship badges:
38. Sharpshooter — 39. Marksman — 40. Pistol Expert — 41. Expert Rifleman

section came under very heavy fire from the enemy.

York, who was the only surviving non-commissioned officer along with seven men, knocked out one machine gun. Then, crawling forward alone, York tried to locate the rest of the machine-guns, which immediately opened up on him. Without hesitation, York returned the fire deliberately, picking off the machine-gunners one by one as their heads appeared when they took aim at him. With his amazing marksmanship, he killed ten in this way. Hoping to overpower him, six Germans leapt out of their trench, but they got no further. York shot the lot and the now demoralised Germans hoisted the white flag and surrendered. Corporal York had silenced thirty-five machine-guns. The facts are incontestible, and Marshal Foch described the exploit as the greatest ever achieved by any soldier of the Allies. York, a worthy successor to Davy Crockett—another man from Tennessee, was awarded the Congressional Medal of Honor, the highest United States decoration for bravery. This decoration is only given for 'extraordinary heroism in connexion with military operations' and only 95 awards were made in the Great War.

The estimates of the total losses of the AEF vary. General March, the Chief of Staff, put them at 50,000 but the War Department gave a figure of 126,000. Other sources put the figure at anything from 60,000 to 75,029. This last figure seems nearest to the truth, but whatever the actual losses may have been the U.S.A. made a very great sacrifice.

The Portuguese Expeditionary Force

The part that the Portuguese played in the Great War is generally forgotten, although they lost nearly 8,000 men in the Flanders mud. Even important works tend to overlook them.

Germany declared war on Portugal on 9 March 1916 but, even before then, Portugal had been forced to send reinforcements to Angola which had been invaded by the Germans.

A Portuguese Expeditionary Force, under the command of General Fernao Tamaquini, sailed for France in 1917. It was armed and equipped largely by the British. The uniform was blue-grey and the men were armed with a ·256 in Mauser rifle.

There had been compulsory military service since 1887, and a law introduced in 1911 had ordained that a Portuguese citizen might enlist

PORTUGUESE ARMY

1–2. Foot soldiers, service dress — 3. Lieutenant
Badges of rank: Other Ranks (worn on the shoulder):
4. Soldier, 1st class — 5. Second Corporal — 6. First Corporal — 7. Second Sergeant — 8. First Sergeant — 9. Warrant Officer
Badges of rank: Officers (worn on the cuff):
10. Probationary Second Lieutenant — 11. Second Lieutenant — 12. Lieutenant — 13. Captain — 14. Major — 15. Lieutenant-Colonel — 16. Colonel — 17. General
Arm of Service badges (worn on the collar and the cap):
18. Engineers — 19. Sappers and Miners — 20. Bridging Troops — 21. Infantry — 22. Garrison Artillery — 23. Search-lights — 24. Field Artillery — 25. Signals — 26. Cavalry — 27. Transportation Troops — 28. Rough-riders — 29. Administrative Service Reserve — 30. Air Observers — 31. Engineer Reserve — 32. Pharmacists — 33. Machine-gunners — 34. Garrison Signals — 35. Submarine Miners — 36. Balloon Service — 37. Pilots — 38. Musicians — 39. Medical Service — 40. Veterinary Service — 41. Administrative Service — 42. Medical Service Reserve — 43. Military Secretariat — 44. Motor Transport Service — 45. Artillery Reserve — 46. Wireless Telegraphists

77

at the age of seventeen years and that he was liable to recall to the colours up to the age of forty-five years. The army consisted of an active force, a reserve and a militia.

The Portuguese Army did not march through Paris: it went straight into the line. The locals thought they were Serbs and the newspapers ignored them. The harsh winter made them suffer terribly because they came from a gentler climate, but their good morale and their ability to adapt themselves to conditions enabled them to match up to their British and French comrades in arms.

The bulk of the contingent came either from the mountain country or were fishermen and both types, calm and resolute, endured the miseries of the trenches with remarkable stoicism. They stood their ground in the face of heavy German attacks, contrary to the Germans' expectations. The British and French leaders were always generous in their praise of the Portuguese, but today that praise sounds faint when one considers the confusion and amazement that these unhappy men must have felt on finding themselves suddenly transported from the quiet and the sunshine of their native land to the pandemonium of Neuve-Église or the Lys.

The Serbian Infantry

In 1914, the Serbian Army consisted principally of infantry and was drawn mostly from men of the mountains or from the peasants, who were well-trained as a result of their continued struggle against the Turks and whom they had just beaten in the Balkan War of 1912.

Although Serbia had practically doubled her territory, she had not come out of the war unscathed. The army, in particular, had exhausted its reserves and the men were a sorry-looking lot in their tattered uniforms. Nevertheless it was still a force to be reckoned with, as the Serbs were intensely patriotic. The whole army, some fourteen divisions, had been issued with service dress in 1912.

We have already dealt with the opening of the campaign in 1914 in the chapter on Austria. During this, in addition to her losses in battle, the Serbian Army suffered a very severe typhus epidemic, which the newspapers of the day blamed Austria-Hungary for.

The Serbs put up an heroic resistance, children and old men, as well as women, were often to be seen fighting in the ranks of the regular army. Under the leadership of General Putnik, the whole nation rose up against the invaders. They laid frequent ambushes and, having an excellent eye for country, they proved highly proficient guerillas. The only form of transport was the

SERBIAN INFANTRY: SERVICE DRESS

1. Foot soldier (1914–16) — 2. Foot soldier, Army of Salonika, wearing French uniform — 3. Foot soldier, winter dress (1914–16) — 4–6. Equipment — 7. French 'Adrian' steel helmet, with badge of Serbian Royal Arms — 8. Rifle and charger

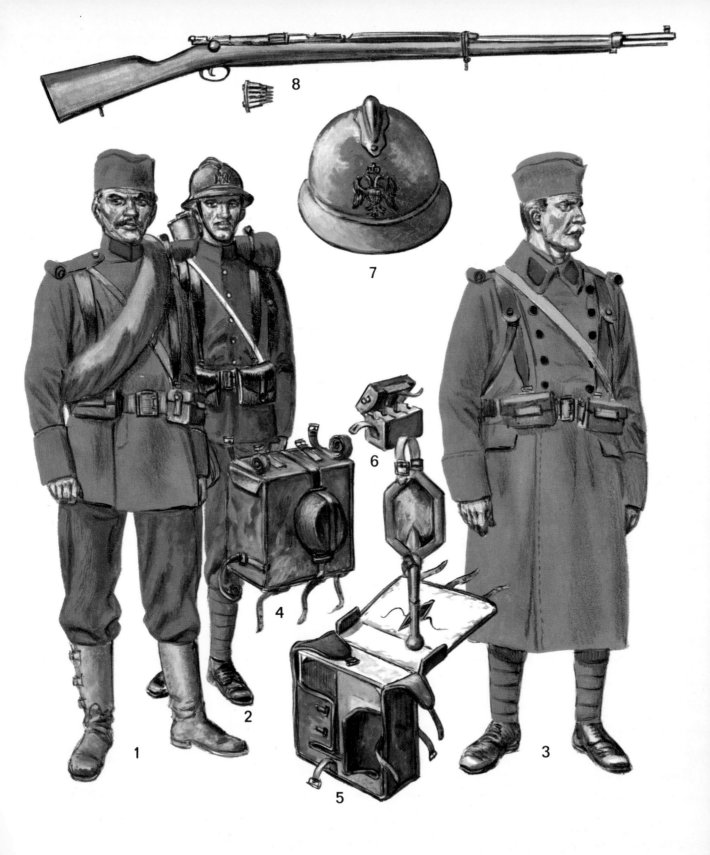

1

2

3

4

5

6

7

8

L. & F. FUNCKEN

bullock-cart, which was the only type suitable to the rough Serbian roads of those days.

On 6 October 1915, the German and Austrian forces and the Bulgarians launched a heavy offensive in the north and in the south-east. In order to avoid being surrounded and wiped out, the gallant army had to retreat over the mountains of Albania where they endured terrible privations, the men dying of hunger and cold on the frozen roads. By a superhuman effort, King Peter and his fellows in misfortune managed to reach the Adriatic and 110,000 men were able to join the Allies. British and French warships took them over to Corfu, where the French had set up a camp in the valley of the Vasilica which gives on to the bay of Salonika[33]. Rested and re-equipped, they were ready to take the field once more in 1916.

Their uniforms, in which they had achieved such glory, were beyond repair and were replaced by French uniforms of horizon-blue or khaki. They adopted the French 'Adrian' steel helmet, with the Serbian Royal Arms as the badge. In the engagements and operations that followed, this new army proved itself to be of the highest order and Serbia lost 369,000 men in the four years of relentless struggle.

Montenegro

Montenegro, now one of the six constituent Republics of Yugoslavia, was a sovereign independent state in 1914 that had been ruled by King Nicolas I since 1860. The Montenegrins stood by their Serbian allies and fought courageously, but their ill-equipped army, barely 40,000 strong, was overwhelmed by the combined forces of the Germans, Austrians and Bulgarians after the Serbian retreat. The Montenegrin Army capitulated on 25 January 1916, but not before they had aroused admiration of the German Field Marshal August von Mackensen[34] and the Austrian General Kövess. The Montenegrins lost some 3,000 dead. King Nicolas I took refuge in Italy, and later went to France where he died in 1921.

At the end of the War, Serbian troops and bands of partisans occupied Montenegro, where they set up a National Assembly which deposed the elderly King and united the country with the new Kingdom of the Serbs, Croats and Slovenes (Jugoslavia).

Greece

Although Greece set herself up as a neutral, King Constantine who was Danish by birth with a Russian mother, leant heavily towards the German side. Indeed, Kaiser Wilhelm II was his brother-in-law and had shown him considerable affection. These family ties did not, however, prevent the unofficial landing of a British and French force at

33 This is not the Salonika where the British Army fought during this war; that one was in Macedonia.
34 Field Marshal von Mackensen had been the Professor in Military History to Kaiser Wilhelm II. After the war, he was in favour of the German Army allying itself to the Nazis.

MONTENEGRO, GREECE AND SERBIA

Montenegro:
1–2. Officer and Private, Royal Guard (known also as *perianiks*) — 3–4. Infantry, in service dress — 10. Order of Danilo I, 4th Class — 11. Medal for Bravery
Greece:
5–6. Foot soldiers, before Greece came into the War — 7–8. Foot soldiers, after Greece came in, wearing items of British and French equipment
Serbia:
9. Gold Obilitch Medal for Bravery

1

2

9

3

4

10

5

6

11

7

8

Salonika, an exploit that was destined to give rise to unimagined complications. Double-faced as ever, King Constantine engineered the surrender of the Greek garrison of Cavalla, a port to the east of Salonika, to the German and Bulgarian troops in 1916, thus placing the Allies in direct contact with the Central Powers. There are photographs that show the Greek troops marching out of Cavalla under arms and these curious prisoners of war continued to draw their pay in Germany.

However, this time the Greek King had overstepped the mark and the Allies, having halted the German-Bulgarian offensive, forced King Constantine to abdicate in favour of his younger son Alexander, who was twenty-four years old.

This was on 12 June 1917 and Greece declared war on the Central Powers a few days later. Her troops took part in the operations in Macedonia where they played an important role in the final offensive in 1918. Their losses amounted to 12,000.

Upon the premature death of King Alexander in 1920 and the fall of the Venizelos Government, King Constantine was restored to the throne. He immediately involved his country in a catastrophic war against Turkey. This monarch, who styled himself the Executioner of the Bulgarians or, more pacifically, as the Saviour of Greece after the Balkan War of 1912–13, was no strategist unfortunately and the Army forced him to abdicate in 1922. He died in 1923.

The Japanese Army

During the nineteenth century, the Japanese Army underwent a metamorphosis, passing from the phase of the matchlock musket to that of the magazine rifle. Owing to their policy of isolation, the Japanese never knew the flintlock but moved forward to percussion weapons as a result of contact with the Americans in 1850.

After the Russo-Japanese War of 1904–5, the Japanese Army was armed and equipped like any European army. When Japan declared war on Germany on 23 August 1914, the service dress of the Army was a brownish khaki. The jacket was single-breasted with five dull buttons and a stand collar. The head-dress was of the British type with a scarlet band, the badge was a five-pointed yellow star. On the collar, there was a swallow-tailed patch, varying in colour according to the arm of the service: red for infantry, green for cavalry, yellow for artillery, brown for engineers and flying corps, and light blue for supplies.

The badges of rank were worn on scarlet stripes

running from front to back at the point of the shoulder. For ranks above corporal, the stars were gilt, as were also the numerals and badges on the collar patches.

The equipment compared favourably with the best European patterns. Most of the rifles were of the Arisaka 1905-pattern, ·245 in, and like most rifles of less than ·276 in, not very powerful. The officers carried automatic pistols of the Nambu 1905 Mark I pattern, ·315 in, although the official weapon was a ·354 in revolver, type 26, that dated

JAPANESE ARMY: SERVICE DRESS

1. Officer — 2–4. Foot soldiers — 5–6. Subaltern Officers — 7. Foot soldier, winter dress — 8. Arisaka rifle, bayonet and charger — 9. Nambu pistol, Type 14, 8-mm
Collar-patches:
10. Infantry — 11. Armoured Troops — 12. Air Service (the patch is of the colour for Engineers)

from 1893. The Nambu pistol derived its name from its inventor, Colonel Kisiru Nambu, and was as well-known as the German Luger in the Second World War. The machine-gun was the Hotchkiss, first of all the 1900-pattern, then the 1914-pattern, both adapted to fire ·245 in ammunition. Colonel Nambu produced a third pattern, which was only a modification of the Hotchkiss.

Based on the numbers involved in the Russo-Japanese War, the probable effective strength of the Japanese Army in 1914 was about 360,000, as the Japanese objectives did not call for any special effort.

It should be borne in mind that the Japanese was a first-class soldier and was led by officers who were convinced of their divine origins and of their incontestable superiority over all other races. This naïve assumption was not something that the authors deduced, but the genuine belief of the Japanese officers of both World Wars. With men of this calibre, and, of course, with limited objectives, Japan was able to make a valuable contribution to the Allied cause. Her first attack was upon the German-leased port of Tsingtao, or Kiaochow, in Northern China. They blockaded the port on 2 September 1914 and, after nineteen days of fighting, they invested the colony. Reinforced by the British, they made the final assault with two divisions on 22 September 1914. The German garrison held out until 7 November, when it finally capitulated.

Apart from a few cruisers which appeared in the Mediterranean in 1917–18 to help combat the German submarines, the Japanese took part in no further operations except in Russia, where they landed at Vladivostok in July 1918 in order to protect the Trans-Siberian Railway against the Russian revolutionaries.

Of all the countries that took part in the First World War, without doubt Japan came off best in relation to her losses. She extended her sphere of influence and improved her economy, at the cost of some 300 dead.

JAPANESE ARMY: IDENTIFICATIONS

Badges of rank:
1. Soldier, 2nd Class — 2. Soldier, 1st Class — 3. Corporal — 4. Sergeant — 5. Staff-Sergeant — 6. Sergeant-Major — 7. Warrant Officer — 8. Second Lieutenant — 9. Lieutenant — 10. Captain — 11. Major — 12. Lieutenant-Colonel — 13. Colonel — 14. Major-General — 15. Lieutenant-General — 16. General — 17. Chief Gaoler — 18. Gaoler
Arm badges:
20. Bugler — 21. Carpenter — 22. Tailor — 23. Bootmaker — 24. Armourer — 25. Blacksmith — 26. Corporal, Acting Sergeant — 27. Good Conduct Badge
Collar badges:
28. Musician — 29. Tank crew — 30. Taiwan (Formosa) Infantry Regiment — 31. Potential Non-commissioned Officer — 32. Supplementary Reserve Officer — 33. Cadet — 34. Pilot — 35. Independent Battalion

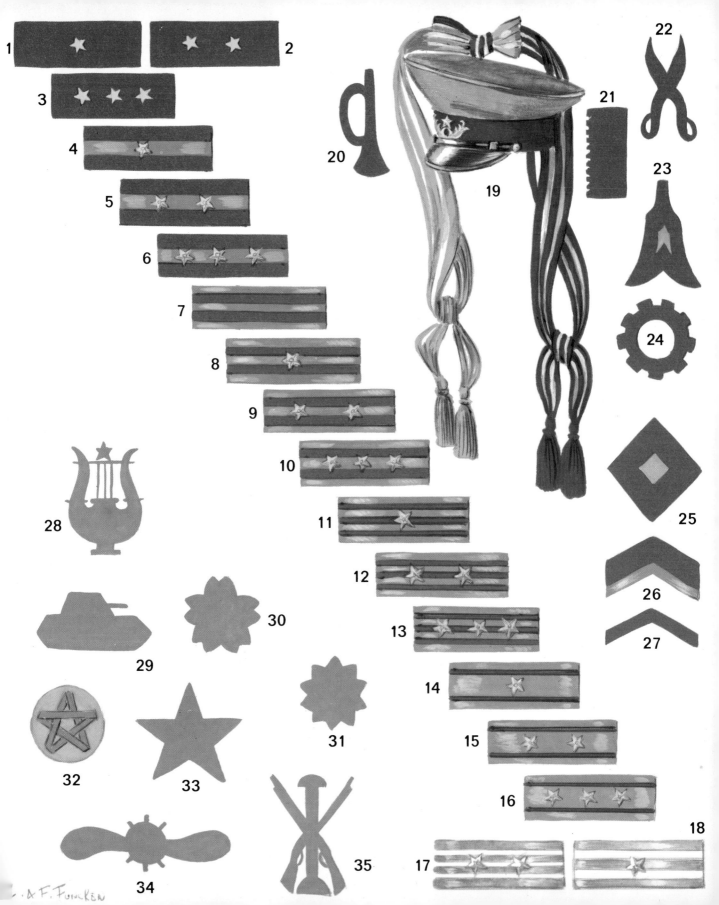

A.F.FUNCKEN

The Romanian Infantry

After the victorious Russian offensive under General Broussilov in the summer of 1915, Romania decided to come in on the side of the Allies against the Central Powers. Right from the start of the war, the country had been sitting on the fence as either side could offer her substantial territorial gains. Moreover, Germany and Austria-Hungary had signed a secret treaty with King Carol I in 1883. As an Hohenzollern Prince, his sympathies were with those of his own race[35].

Much to the King's displeasure, the Council of State decided in favour of provisional neutrality which he took to mean that, in the end, the country would join the Allies. This breach of the code of honour which required him to abide by his agreements further undermined the King's failing health, and he died in October 1914. This, coupled with the unexpected French victory on the Marne, strengthened the pro-Allies faction. The new King, a nephew of his predecessor, was crowned under the name of Ferdinand I on 11 October 1914[36].

King Ferdinand had been elected Crown Prince in 1889, but his uncle had excluded him from the Court and from his secret political activities. Shy and self-effacing, the Crown Prince devoted his mind to botany, a science of which he acquired a great knowledge. These peace-loving studies, however, did not prevent his taking an active interest in the reorganisation of the army and he had fought in the campaign against the Bulgarians in 1913 as Commander-in-Chief.

In 1893, Ferdinand had married Princess Mary of Edinburgh, who was a grand-child both of Queen Victoria of Great Britain and of the Tzar Alexander II of Russia, and this played an important part in his ultimate decision. He had to hold out against the pressure of the pro-German faction who were emboldened by the fact that he was himself a German by birth. Nevertheless, he took the only course compatible with his dignity as King, even though it forced him to offer an affront to his family and to break all ties with them.

The reaction of the Hohenzollerns to this betrayal was swift. The name of Ferdinand was erased from the Family Tree, thus killing him genealogically, and the Court of the Principality of Sigmaringen at once went into mourning! To finish the job, Kaiser Wilhelm II, King of Prussia and German Emperor, informed the renegade that he had been expelled from the House Order. King Ferdinand never renounced his name and, for all of this storm of maledictions, two years later he was the only Hohenzollern who still could use his family name, for all the rest had been deprived of the right by decree of the victorious Allies.

Romania's entry into the War brought the Allies, albeit with some delay, thirteen divisions.

35 Carol I, the founder of the dynasty, was born at Sigmaringen in 1839, a prince of the House of Hohenzollern, and was crowned King of Romania in 1881.
36 Ferdinard I, the second son of Carol I's elder brother, Prince Leopold of Hohenzollern-Sigmaringen and the Infanta Antonia of Portugal, was born at Sigmaringen in 1865. His father's pretensions to the Spanish throne were a cause of the Franco-Prussian War of 1870–1.

ROMANIAN INFANTRY: SERVICE DRESS, 1912

1. Infantry of the Line — 2. *Chasseur à Pied* — 3. A Regimental Mascot: an Ox — 4. Regimental Colour — 5. Major

Unfortunately, these were poorly armed, and only eight of them had machine-guns. The Romanian Army was armed with the Mannlicher 1893-pattern, ·245 in rifle which had a five-round magazine.

In 1912, a blue-grey service dress had been adopted, which was similar in colour to the Austrian uniform, but by 1916 it had become horizon-blue in colour. At this time, a steel helmet of the French pattern was taken into use.

On 27 August 1916, Romania declared war on Austria, and, on the following day, her army crossed the Carpathians in company with the Russians under Broussilov. The German reaction was instantaneous and shattering. The required number of divisions were withdrawn from the Western Front and, in conjunction with the Bulgarians, Romania was encircled as had Serbia been in 1915. The intervention of the Bulgarians, against whom Romania had carefully not declared war in the hope that they would not intervene, made sure of the defeat of the Romanian Army. Transylvania was evacuated and the Romanians were driven back to the east of the Carpathians, unable to resist the German, Austrian, Bulgarian and Turkish forces that surrounded them.

The Allies, divided as how best to intervene, finally left the Romanians to their fate. It is true, of course, that the British and the French, and the Russians too, had their own problems. All the same, the twenty-five Romanian divisions that opposed forty divisions of the enemy acquitted themselves well. Among the enemy, there was a young lieutenant from Württemberg, Erwin Rommel, who was destined to become famous, twenty-five years later.

The Russian reinforcements proved too weak to help the Romanians whose position worsened daily and dragged on for three months. On 3 December, the Germans broke through and Bucharest fell. The Romanian Army made an orderly retreat, in bitter weather, across the Moldavian Plain to the temporary shelter of the river Putna and the river Sereth.

The winter of 1916–17 proved a gruelling one and the army was decimated by typhus. Nevertheless, with the help of a French Military Mission under General Berthelot, King Ferdinand managed to rally his army at Jassy so successfully that he launched an offensive with seventeen divisions in the summer and had some success initially. This, however, was short-lived for the Russian 4th Army went over to the revolutionaries and laid down its arms, the German General von Mackensen was then able to knock out the Romanian Army for good and all, though not without a fortnight's resistance.

The fall of Kerensky in Russia, followed shortly by the signing of the Treaty of Brest-Litovsk between Germany and Russia, sounded the knell for Romania and, alone and deserted on 9 December 1917, she signed a separate armistice at Focsani. Romania had lost more than 300,000 dead. Needless to say, Romania was not allowed to get away with it. On 7 May 1918, the Central Powers forced King Ferdinand to sign the Treaty of Bucharest, which deprived Romania of vast tracts of country and several strategic points. Furthermore, she was systematically plundered of her oil, her flocks and her timber.

ROMANIAN INFANTRY:
SERVICE DRESS, 1916–19

1. Lieutenant — 2. Captain — 3. General of Division — 4. Lieutenant — 5–6. Infantry of the Line, field service marching order — 7. *Chasseur à Pied* — 8. *Chasseur à Pied*, with French 'Adrian' steel helmet — 9. Infantry of the Line, battle order — 10. Officer's waist-belt — 11. Haversack and entrenching-tool — 12. Valise — 13. Underside of valise — 14. Bayonet-frog

Fortunately, the King refused to co-operate in putting this disgraceful treaty into effect, and showed his people that he identified himself wholly with them. One of the clauses required the immediate expulsion of General Berthelot and the three hundred officers of his Mission and stipulated that no one should see them off at the railway station, whence they were to depart by night. In the event, as the train drew out, the General was saluted by the King, the Queen and their six children, all of whom wished to pay tribute to the part the Mission had played in helping Romania to uphold her ideals. King Ferdinand had stood firm and, when the Central Powers collapsed on 9 November 1918, he once again declared war on them although only as a gesture. The King's re-entry into Bucharest was triumphant. The last of the Hohenzollerns had deserved well of his adopted land.

ROMANIAN ARMY: IDENTIFICATIONS

Columns show respectively, full-dress collar, full-dress shoulder-straps, service-dress shoulder-straps and full-dress caps for each rank of officer:
1, 10, 19, 41. General of Army Corps — 2, 11, 20, 42. General of Division — 3, 12, 21, 43. General of Brigade — 4, 13, 22, 44. Colonel — 5, 14, 23, 45. Lieutenant-Colonel — 6, 15, 24, 46. Major — 7, 16, 25, 47. Captain — 8, 17, 26, 48. Lieutenant — 9, 18, 27, 49. Second Lieutenant
Other ranks:
28. Warrant Officer, 1st Class — 29. Warrant Officer, 2nd Class — 30. Sergeant — 31. Corporal — 32. Soldier, 1st Class — 33, 40. Private, Infantry of the Line and Frontier Guards — 39. Private, *Chasseurs à Pied*
Staff Officers (in each case, a Major is shown):
34. I Army Corps — 35. II Army Corps — 36. III Army Corps — 37. IV Army Corps — 38. V Army Corps
Miscellaneous:
50. Cockade on cap — 51. General Officer's service dress cap — 52. Lieutenant's service dress cap — 53. Cap badge in form of Royal Cypher of King Ferdinand — 54. French pattern steel helmet, with Royal Cypher badge — 55. Medal for Military Valour

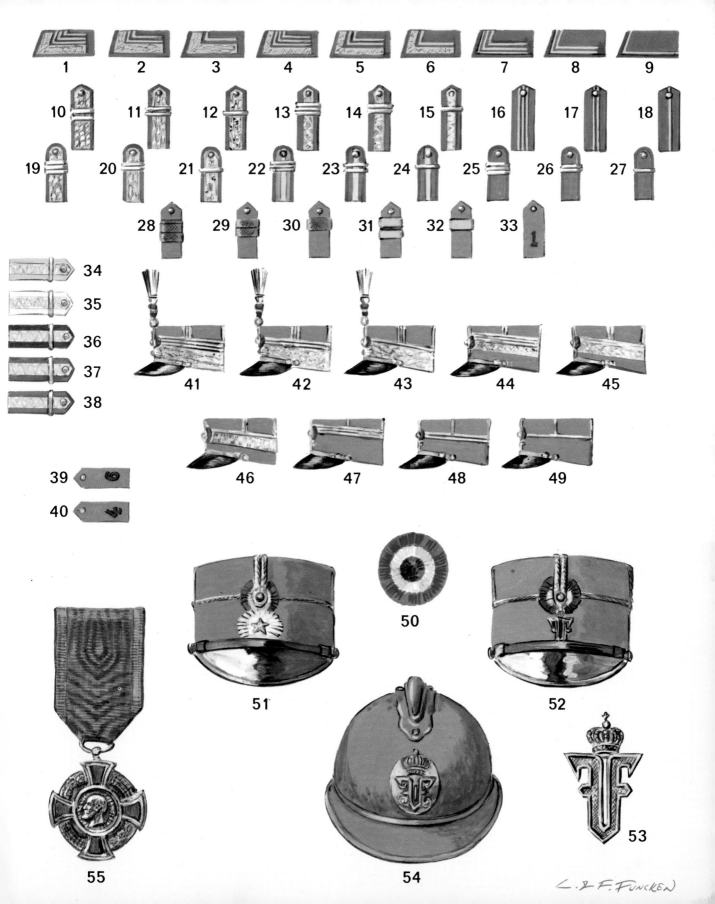

The Polish Volunteers

When the First World War broke out, the Polish political groups reacted in different ways, some siding with Russia, some with Austria-Hungary, but disagreeing among themselves. It must be borne in mind that, at this time, Poland was not an independent state but was largely in Russia with small areas in Prussia and Austria.

Upon mobilisation, the Germans called the inhabitants of Posen (or Poznan) to the colours and drafted them to regiments as required, but in areas under Russian and Austrian control, the Poles were allowed to form their own Legions of Volunteers who would fight alongside the regular troops of the occupying powers. The Polish patriots saw in this the means of gaining some measure of autonomy and, perhaps, the liberation of their country, but neither Russia nor Austria realised this. The question did not arise in the area occupied by the Prussians, for they were wholly impervious to the aspirations of the population that they had enslaved.

Thus three armies sprang up in Poland, one on the Austro-Hungarian frontier, one on the Russian and, finally, after the Germans had also allowed the Poles to form volunteers, one on the German frontier.

In all three countries, the Polish Legions were used without any consideration and were sent on the most dangerous missions, in the secret hope that they would be wiped out after having made themselves useful! Together, the Polish Legions numbered some 2,000,000 men fighting for freedom, but fighting on different sides. The Russian element was the strongest with about 1,200,000, and the German and Austrian elements each had about 350,000.

There were many Poles living throughout the world. Many immediately joined the French Foreign Legion and were in action from the start. Then volunteers came from everywhere, particularly the U.S.A. and eventually, a separate army was formed. In 1918, this had a strength of three divisions.

On the Eastern Front, the German and Austrian Polish Legions mutinied and joined the Russians after the Tzar abdicated. These Legions formed the framework of the Polish Army, when Poland achieved independence and unity in 1920.

The Czechoslovak Volunteers

In 1914, Czechoslovakia was part of the Austro-Hungarian Empire. On the outbreak of the War, the Czechs and the Slovaks in the Austrian Army deserted *en masse* to the Russians, where they formed a contingent of 92,000 men. In France and in Italy, volunteers and former prisoners of war founded a Slovak corps of 12,000 and a Czech corps of 24,000 men. Thanks to these men and to the energy of Tomas Masaryk (1850–1937), the Republic of Czechoslovakia was founded in 1918.

Poles: 1. 1st Brigade, Pilsudski Legion — 2–3. Polish Volunteers in France — 4. Polish Volunteer in the French service
Czechs: 5. Battalion colour-bearer, Czech Volunteers in the French service — 6. Czech Volunteer in the Italian service — 7. Czech Volunteer in the Russian service

1   2   3   4

5   6   7

L & F. Funcken

PART TWO

THE CENTRAL POWERS

The German Infantry

In 1914, Germany formed an homogeneous nation. The idea of a Germany, rather than a mass of German States, had started to grow during the humiliations of the Napoleonic Wars. Between 1870 and the beginning of the twentieth century, the process of cohesion was completed. Industry was built up, there was a phenomenal increase in the birth rate (a million a year), and this gradually persuaded Germany of her claim to greatness. She needed to find new markets, if she were to feed her expanding population and preserve her world standing, so Germany started looking for colonies, a thing she had not previously bothered about much.

Nothing more was needed to make 'Pan-Germanism' flourish, for this would show the world that Germans were a chosen race, destined to be the spiritual leaders of all other nations. The accession of Kaiser Wilhelm II in 1888 gave 'Pan-Germanism' just the champion it needed.

The young Emperor, the favourite grandson of Queen Victoria of Great Britain, was soon to become the most universally hated man in the world and was the first to be branded officially as a war criminal[37]. No one has ever been treated more brutally by cartoonists and journalists. Even today, mention of the Kaiser conjures up the picture of the vulture with a spiked helmet and a twisted moustache hovering over millions of graves. The picture expressed the detestation felt by all decent people for a nation, drunk with pride,

which believed that might was right and, as the man principally responsible, Wilhelm II became

GERMAN INFANTRY: IDENTIFICATIONS
1. Rifleman (1914) (the wearing of beards was discontinued after the first winter of the War) — 2. *Chasseur* of the Guard, in service dress with upright collar — 3. Full dress tunic and helmet — 4–5. Service dress jacket, with turn-down collar — 6. Service dress jacket, with upright collar
Service dress caps:
7. Officer, Infantry of the Line (1914) — 8. Other ranks, Infantry of the Line — 9. Other ranks, *Chasseurs* — 10. Other ranks, Fusiliers of the Guard — 11. Other ranks, Foot Guards — 12. Other ranks, Guards Machine-gunners — 13. Other ranks, Bavarian *Chasseurs* — 14. Stretcher-bearers
Cockades:
The upper cockade on the service-dress cap was in the German colours, black-white-red. The lower cockade was that of the State to which the unit belonged.

(a)	Prussia	(b)	Bavaria
(c)	Saxony	(d)	Württemberg
(e)	Baden	(f)	Hessen
(g)	Mecklenburg	(h)	Oldenburg
(i)	Brunswick	(j)	Anhalt
(k)	Saxe-Weimar	(l)	Saxe-Coburg
(m)	Saxe-Meiningen	(n)	Saxe-Altenburg
(o)	Lippe	(p)	Schaumburg-Lippe
(q)	Waldeck	(r)	Schwarzburg-Rudolstadt
(s)	Reuss		
(t)	Schwarzburg-Sonderhausen	(u)	Hamburg
(w)	Lübeck	(v)	Bremen

Bayonet-knots:
15. Machine-gunner: the knot consists of —

A.	the strap	D.	the crown
B.	the slide	E.	the fringe
C.	the body		

In the Infantry, the Battalions and Companies were distinguished by the colours of B, C and D, as follows:
C indicated the Battalion: 1st, white; 2nd, red; 3rd, yellow.
B and D were the same colour and indicated the Company, there being four Companies in each Battalion:
1, 5, and 9 Companies–white — 2, 6, and 10 Companies–red — 3, 7, and 11 Companies–yellow — 4, 8, and 12 Companies–blue

---

37 The Treaty of Versailles, 1919, held him responsible for the war but the Dutch government refused to extradite him for trial. He lived at Doorn near Utrecht, in Holland until his death in 1941.

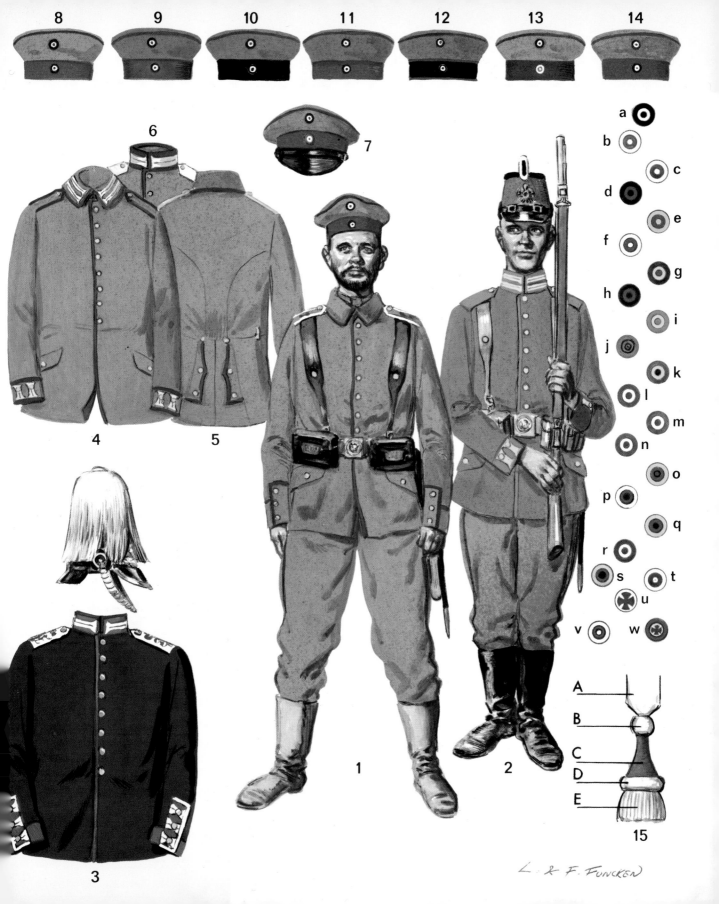

L. & F. Funcken

the personification. He was spared nothing: if he tried to conceal his withered left arm, that was proof that he was degenerate. In fact, this disability was the result of an injury at birth and there is a sketch of the Kaiser out shooting, with his gun to his shoulder and firing one-handed, in the presence of a number of onlookers. But these were not gentle times, as Germany herself had just plainly demonstrated.

A good husband and a good father, Wilhelm of Prussia succeeded his father, Kaiser Frederick III, who had reigned only a few months. Suddenly becoming Emperor and thus enjoying unlimited power, he passed from being justly proud of his country's achievements to adopt a haughty and conceited attitude as the head of a race destined to rule the world. The illustrated weeklies in the years immediately preceding the conflagration of 1914 show him in numerous different uniforms; so many that one can only conclude that he had a mania for fancy dress. His wardrobe contained hundreds of uniforms as well as numerous examples of period costume. Megalomania was becoming apparent. He set himself up as a dramatist and wrote an unbelievably dreary play, he painted, he did some drawing but, more than anything else, he showed a remarkable skill as a propagandist. It was he who organised the intensive propaganda that was to cast a spell over his people who became positively devoted to the *régime*.

Under the Kaiser's impulse, 'Pan-Germanism' grew apace, influencing every detail of daily life. In the schools, Greek and Latin were ousted in favour of German for the study of dead languages was considered a waste of time. The Kaiser took the greatest interest in the Army: by paying attention to every little detail, he contrived to turn every ceremonial parade to the enhancing of the spirit of Germany.

The spectre of war grew larger. Ever since 1905, the Kaiser had been trying to pick a quarrel with France over the Moroccan question; in 1911 at the risk of starting the blaze, he had sent a gunboat to Agadir in order to force the French to share her conquests with him. Finally, Germany secured some territory in Central Africa. The arms race speeded up, and the stage was set for the tragedy of 1914–18.

STRATEGY AND ORGANISATION

In 1894, France and Russia had signed a Treaty of Alliance and, three years later, Germany had formulated a plan to deal with the eventuality of a war on two fronts. This plan had been drawn up by General von Schlieffen and had been modified to suit changing conditions by his successor, General von Moltke.

On the assumption that any French attack would be launched against the Lorraine frontier, the German General Staff proposed to overrun Belgium in order to encircle the French Army and force it into the area bounded by the Moselle, the Jura and the Swiss frontier where it could be annihilated. This action would involve the violation of Belgium and would bring down the wrath of England but, if action were taken speedily, the war would be over in a few weeks before Britain

GERMAN INFANTRY, 1914–18

1. Foot soldier in full equipment — 2. Details of the valise —
A. pocket for clean underwear
C. pocket for rations
B. sleeve for bivouac
D. pocket for necessaries and iron ration
3. Mess-tin and mug — 4. Pick-axe and entrenching tool — 5. Mauser rifle, bayonet and charger — 6. *Pickelhaube* (with and without cover) right-hand side with German cockade (Cf. Fig. 17) — 6a. *Pickelhaube*, left-hand side with State cockade of Saxe-Weimar — 7. Waist-belt buckle, with motto *Gott mit uns*
Cockades:
8. Prussia — 9. Bavaria — 10. Saxony — 11. Württemberg — 12. Baden — 13. Hesse — 14. Mecklenburg — 15. Oldenburg — 16. Brunswick — 17. German Empire — 18. Shoulder-straps, service dress: (a) 1st Foot Guards, 5th Foot Guards, 5th Guard Grenadiers; (b) 2nd Foot Guards; (c) 3rd Foot Guards, Guard Fusiliers; (d) 4th Foot Guards; (e) 1st Guard Grenadiers; (f) 2nd Guard Grenadiers; (g) 3rd Guard Grenadiers; (h) 4th Guard Grenadiers; (i) 45th Infantry Regiment; (j) 36th Infantry Regiment; (k) 61st Infantry Regiment; (l) 19th Infantry Regiment; (m) 181st Infantry Regiment; (n) 6th Grenadier Regiment; (o); (p); (q) 1st Jägers; (r); (s); (t) 5th Pioneer Battalion

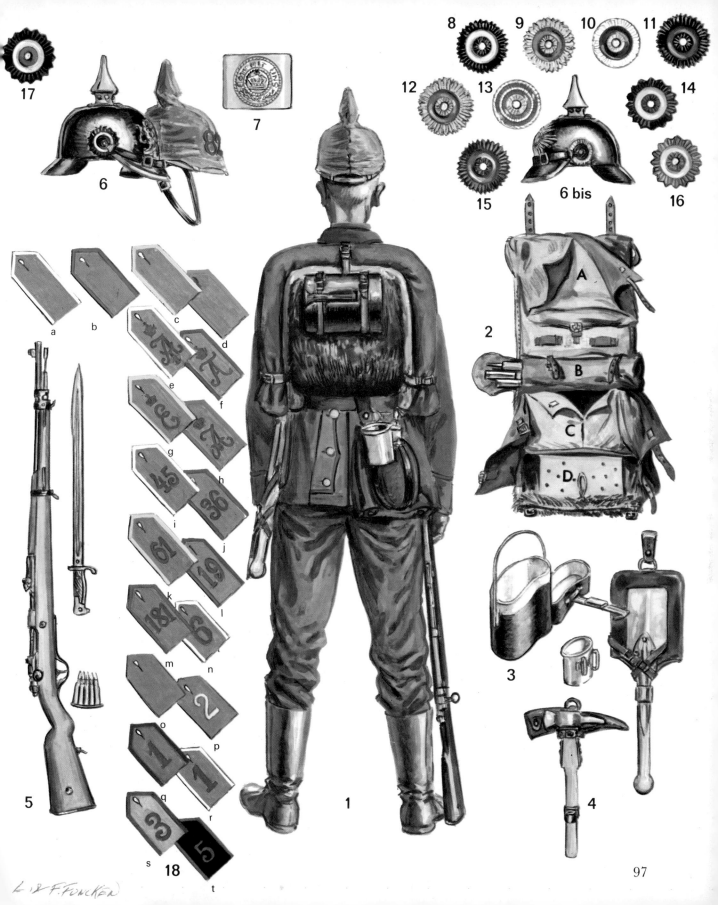

97

L. & F. FUNCKEN

could do anything except on a diplomatic level. Germany took little account of Russia after her defeat by Japan in 1905: she could be dealt with after France had been knocked out.

The French plan, known as Plan XVII, was designed to deal with an attack on the Franco-German frontier and, naïvely, considered any advance through Belgium as purely hypothetical, except perhaps through the Ardennes. Germany however had no scruples when it came to violating Belgian neutrality.

The French General Staff did not place any great reliance on the army reserve but the Germans, on the other hand, had taken great care that their reserve divisions should be trained so that they could be of immediate use. There were eighty-one divisions, active and reserve, in all.

Military service was compulsory, the first two years were spent with the colours and the next five years on the reserve. This was followed by varying periods in the militia, of which there were three classes, and liability to call-up did not end until the age of forty-five. The role of the militia was seen as garrison duty in occupied enemy territory. A division was 17,000 strong, of which four-fifths were infantry, consisting of two brigades, each of two regiments.

THE UNIFORM

The principal characteristic of the German foot soldier was his spiked helmet, the *Pickelhaube*, which strange as it may seem, was of Danish origin. This was made of moulded leather, painted black and was fitted with white-metal or brass mountings. The badge was either an Eagle or some other heraldic device and was in silver or gilt for the officers. A bar of the same metal ran from the boss supporting the spike to the edge of the back peak. The spike could be removed and, in some regiments in review order, it was replaced by a black or a white plume. The chin-straps were of black leather or of metal scales. The

right-hand side fastening was in the form of the German cockade, the left-hand in that of the State whence the regiment came, e.g. Saxony, Württemberg, etc.

The tunic was blue with scarlet facings but, on service, this was replaced by a field-grey uniform that had been introduced in 1910. The *chasseurs* and the machine-gun units, however, wore a bright green uniform. Nevertheless the field-grey uniform retained the various characteristics of the parent States in the form of the piping of the collar, cuffs, shoulder-straps and pockets.

In 1915, a new style of jacket was introduced. This was also field-grey in colour and had a fly-front with a stand-and-fall collar. The shoulder-straps were, for the most part, piped with white and showed the regimental numeral or monogram in red, though there were a number of exceptions. In all cases, the trousers were field-grey.

The following regiments did not have white piping, but piping of the colour shown:

Dark red:

2nd Guards Infantry, 2nd Guards Grenadiers and 8th Grenadiers.

Lemon yellow:

3rd Guards Infantry, 3rd Guards Grenadiers, Guards Fusiliers and 7th to 11th Grenadiers.

Bright blue:

4th Guards Infantry, 4th Guards Grenadiers and 145th Royal Infantry.

Bright green:

114th Infantry

GERMAN INFANTRY, 1914

1–2. Prussian riflemen (1914) — 3–5. Prussian machine-gunners. The leather shoulder-belts were used for carrying the guns and pulling them into position. They gave rise to a legend that the German officers strapped the men to their weapons, so that they would be forced to fight to the last round

99

The Guards Regiments were distinguished by characteristic stripes of lace on the collar and cuffs of the tunic. On the field-grey jacket, these were retained on the collar but in grey, instead of white, and had a coloured light in the middle:

Short double stripe with white light having dark red edges:
1st to 4th Guards Infantry, 1st to 4th Guards Grenadiers, Guards Fusiliers, 89th, 100th, 101st, 109th, 119th and 123rd Grenadiers, 115th Body Guard and Bavarian Infantry.

Long single stripe with white light:
5th Guards Infantry.

Long single stripe with yellow light:
5th Guards Grenadiers.

Long single stripe without light:
80th Fusiliers.

Medium-length single stripe with white light:
1st-6th, 8th and 11th Grenadiers.

Medium-length single stripe with yellow light:
7th Grenadiers.

The regiments wearing stripes on the collar had red stripes on their trousers.

The *Chasseurs* and the *Tirailleurs* had jackets of a greenish hue with the exception of those from Bavaria. The former bright green shoulder-straps, which were too easily visible, were replaced by ones of self material with bright green piping for the *Chasseurs* and black for the *Tirailleurs*. The numerals and monograms were red in both cases. In the Guards Regiments, the stripes on the collar were doubled and of grey with a yellow light. The lumen between the stripes was filled with bright green for the Guards *Chasseurs* and black for the Guards *Tirailleurs*. The buttons were of brass or of white-metal and the trousers had green stripes. The former light grey greatcoats were replaced by ones of field-grey with shoulder-straps like those of the jacket.

The Machine-gunners

The machine-gun detachments who had had a greenish-grey uniform with red trimmings since the outbreak of war, changed little, merely adopting self-coloured facings and dull buttons. We would stress, however, that the jacket introduced in 1915 did not entirely replace the earlier field-grey tunic which, with various modifications, remained in use throughout the Great War.

THE EVOLUTION OF THE HELMET

With the introduction of field-grey, the *Pickelhaube* was fitted with a yellowish-grey cotton cover, on the front of which the regimental numeral was painted in red. Later the colour was changed to green, though some reserve units had always used green. The covers issued to the men were ill-cut but those of the officers were better made.

The helmets themselves provided little protection and their shape betrayed them from a distance even with the covers. The first attempt to solve the problem was to remove the spike. Then an extremely well-designed, but very heavy, steel helmet was introduced, in 1916. In its original form, this had a visor and, including this, the helmet weighed rather over 7 lb. The visor was soon discontinued and all that remained of it were the pivots which were, later mistaken for ventilators. Gradually the steel helmet became a general issue to all front line troops.

GERMAN INFANTRY, 1917–18

1. Foot soldier, in battle order, lightened version — 2. Foot soldier, wearing equipment with water-proof valise — 3. Machine gun, MG, 1908-pattern — 4. Light machine gun, 1908–15-pattern — 5. Foot soldier, in battle order — 6. Officer — 7. Feed belt, for light machine gun (Cf. 4).

THE EQUIPMENT

In 1914, the German infantry was equipped with the 1895-pattern valise, which was made of light brown rawhide bound with undyed leather and fitted with pack-boards to keep it square. It had a waterproof lining and was supported by double braces, one of which was attached to the ammunition pouches while the other passed under the arm and kept the valise in place. The first pair of braces took the weight of the ammunition pouches off the waistbelt, a detail that was a great improvement on the French equipment. The old pouches were of stiff black leather and each held 45 rounds, these were used along with ones of a later and better pattern.

A mess tin and an aluminium mug were attached to the waistbelt, together with a waterbottle. Each company had 115 mixed tools, picks, entrenching-tools and hatchets, which were also carried attached to the waistbelt. The greatcoat was rolled inside a bivouac and was carried in a horseshoe over the top of the valise. A blackened aluminium saucepan completed the equipment.

The German infantryman normally carried three days' rations consisting of biscuits, preserved meat and vegetables, salt and coffee. His total load was equal to that of the French infantryman, so that they were the two most heavily-laden of all the belligerents.

THE WEAPONS

The Rifle

The Mauser 1898-pattern rifle was a magazine rifle, loaded from 5-round chargers. The calibre was ·312 in, and the ball sharp-pointed. The rifle was a little over 4 ft 3 in long without the bayonet and weighed, charged, 9 lb 12 oz. The bayonet had a saw down the back of the blade. This was made the subject of all sorts of horror-stories but was, in fact, intended just for sawing. The rifle had a range similar to that of the French Lebel, but, up to 800 yards, the trajectory was higher.

The Machine-gun

After the Russo-Japanese War, the machine-gun had been accepted as a weapon to be reckoned with and, in the Great War, all the belligerents used it. In 1899, the Germans adopted the Maxim. This had been perfected in 1908 and was to prove one of the deadliest weapons of the war. The calibre was the same as the Mauser rifle, and it had a rate of fire of 450 rounds per minute. The barrel was water-cooled. It had a range comparable with the French machine-gun of about 1,500 yards. The gun team consisted of five men.

GERMAN INFANTRY, 1914–18

1–2. Foot soldiers, in battle order — 3. Officer — 4. Corporal — 5. Body-armour worn in the trenches — 6. Machine-gunner — 7. Assault battalion (1918) — 8. 110th Grenadier Regiment: the spike has been removed from the helmet — 9. Foot soldier, wearing gas-mask (1916–18) — 10. Disc grenade (1914) — 11. Gas grenade: the liquid gas is contained in a porcelain sphere — 12. Stick grenade, of the last pattern — 13. Spherical, fragmentation grenade — 14. Bayonet and scabbard, 1915-pattern
Note. The haversacks carried by 2, 5, and 7 contained grenades

GERMAN ARMY:
IDENTIFICATIONS, 1915 REGULATIONS

General Officers:
1. General Officer (Prussia) in service dress — 2. Field Marshal, in tunic — 9. General Officers' collar and cuffs (in silver, for Bavaria)
Staff:
3. *Aide-de-Camp* to the Emperor, in patrol jacket
Officers:
4. Colonel — 5. Colonel, 8th Grenadiers, in full dress — 6. Lieutenant-Colonel — 7. Major — 8. Captain
Collars and cuffs:
10. Officers, Fusiliers, Grenadiers and Guards Militia; Bavarian *Leib-Regiments* and Mecklenburg Chasseurs. Similar devices in gold are worn by the Foot Guards
Note. A *Leib-Regiment* is one of which the Sovereign is Colonel. There is no exact equivalent, and no translation applicable, in the British Army
11. Officer, 8th Grenadiers — 12. Officer, 5th Grenadiers — 13. Officer, 4th Grenadiers — 14. 1st, 2nd, 3rd and 4th Grenadiers of the Guard.

1 2 3 4 5 6

12 13

7 8 9

11

10

14

L. & F. Funcken

9   10   11

1   2   3   4

L. & F. Funcken

12

13

14

5

6

7

8

It was a sturdy weapon, but heavy. However a light machine-gun, the 1908–15-pattern, was introduced in 1915, which had a butt and a bipod mounting. It was fed by a rotating magazine.

A British eye-witness has stated that the Germans had secretly manufactured 50,000 machine-guns in preparation for the war but in fact, at the outbreak of the war, Germany had 5,000, which was about the same number as the French. Undoubtedly it was the statement of this 'eye-witness', coupled with the more effective use to which the Germans put this new weapon, that gave birth to the legend of the German superiority over France in this respect.

The Grenade

The first type of German grenade was little better than that of the French. It consisted of a discus with six horns which held percussion fuses, and weighed about $12\frac{1}{2}$ oz. It was set off by one of the horns being hit. The next type of grenade was spherical, weighing about $2\frac{1}{4}$ lb. It was set off by a friction-striker and the case fragmented into seventy pieces. Both these grenades, however, only contained a charge of black powder, so that they were of limited effect. More powerful explosives required detonating and, in due course, an ovoid grenade appeared which was similar to the French type. This was soon followed by a stick grenade which was operated by the withdrawal of a pin, when the head left the handle.

A rifle grenade was also tried out, but it was given up because it was too inaccurate and was replaced by a grenade thrower, the projectiles of which were as powerful as a 77 mm shell[38].

38 See Volume II, Artillery.

GERMAN COLONIAL TROOPS

1–2. Corporal and staff-sergeant, Colonial Infantry, East Africa — 3. Officers, South West Africa Police — 4–5. Officer and staff-sergeant, Colonial Infantry, East Africa — 6. East Africa Military Police — 7. Togo Police — 8. Sergeant-Bugler, Colonial Infantry, Cameroons — 9. Staff-Sergeant, Colonial Infantry, Cameroons

The Austro-Hungarian Infantry

The Austro-Hungarian Army, whose remarkable efforts on the Italian Front we have already noticed, had forty-nine infantry divisions in 1914. An infantry regiment consisted of four active battalions and a depot. There were thirty-nine battalions of *Chasseurs*.

The Austro-Hungarian Army was an heterogeneous body: 47% Slav, 29% German-speaking Austrians, 18% Magyar, 5% Romanian and 1% Italian. The liability for military service extended from the age of twenty to that of forty-three years: two years with the colours, eleven years in the reserve and ten years in the local militia. Despite this mixture of races, the men were remarkably loyal to their Emperor although some felt a leaning towards their Russian or Romanian blood-brothers. The corps of officers, on the other hand, was three-quarters composed of Austrians of German stock.

THE UNIFORM

The original service dress of the Austrian Army was of much the same colour as the French horizon blue, but somewhat greyer. It was first introduced in 1908. In 1916, the blue-grey uniform was replaced by one of field-grey, but not so green as the German variety. Up to 1916, the officers wore a black and yellow sash over the waistbelt, a survival from the Napoleonic wars[39]. At the same time, the carrying of the sword on service was discontinued in favour of an ordinary bayonet.

THE WEAPONS

The Rifle

The most widely-used Austrian rifle was the Mannlicher 1895-pattern, ·315 in with a 5-round magazine. This excellent rifle was manufactured at Steyr, a centre of the steel industry, and was also used in the Romanian, Bulgarian and Greek armies. In the Second World War, the Italian army was also armed with the Mannlicher. A carbine of the same type was used by some specialist units, like the Cyclist Companies armed with machine-guns.

The Machine-gun

On an average, there were four machine-guns per regiment, which were Schwarzlose, ·315 in and water-cooled. They were also made at Steyr. The ammunition made a flash, which was easily visible at night and necessitated the use of a flash-eliminator of characteristic design. This is the conical extension of the barrel, shown in the illustration.

The illustrations also show the various details of the equipment of the Austrian infantry. We shall only mention the reserve ammunition pouch which was of distinctive appearance.

39 See *Arms and Uniforms – 18th Century to the Present Day*.

AUSTRIAN INFANTRY, 1914–16

1–2. Foot soldiers, in service dress with full equipment. A lamp for use on the march at night is inserted into the muzzle of the rifle — 3–5. Details of the valise — 6. Haversack and water-bottle — 7. Reserve ammunition pouch, carried at the waist behind — 8. Cooking-pan — 9. Mess-tin — 10. Water-bottle, ½-litre, 1909-pattern — 11. Water-bottle, ·45-litre, 1888-pattern — 12. Details of the cartridge carriers — 13. Waist-belt plate — 14. Waist-belt, outer and under sides

F. FUNCKEN

The Badges of Rank and Identifications

The badges of rank were worn on a collar patch of a distinctive colour. The following table shows the diversity of colours used by the first twenty regiments, out of a total of one hundred and two in existence in 1914, and it will be seen that there were many subtle differences in tone.

Up to the rank of Warrant Officer, the stars were white, for Cadets they were silver-plated and for Junior Officers silver or gilt matching the buttons. For General and Field Officers, the lace on the collar matched the buttons and the stars were of the opposite colour. A Field Marshal wore lace of a special pattern, without stars.

Regiment	Nationality	Distinctive Colour	Buttons
1	German	Deep red	Brass
2	Hungarian	Imperial green	Brass
3	German	Sky blue	White metal
4	German	Sky blue	Brass
5	Hungarian	Pink	Brass
6	Hungarian	Pink	White metal
7	German	Dark brown	White metal
8	German	Grass green	Brass
9	German	Apple green	Brass
10	German	Emerald green	White metal
11	German	Ash	Brass
12	Hungarian	Dark brown	Brass
13	German	Pink	Brass
14	German	Black	Black
15	German	Maroon	Brass
16	Hungarian	Pale yellow	Brass
17	German	Brown red	White metal
18	German	Deep red	White metal
19	Hungarian	Sky blue	White metal
20	German	Lobster pink	White metal

AUSTRIAN ARMY:
BADGES OF RANK AND MISCELLANEOUS

1–2. Soldier and Officer, service dress (1914–16) — 3. Company bugler: his bugle is tuned in F — 4. Bugler of a Mounted Infantry Battalion: his bugle is tuned in A

Note. French bugles are tuned in B-flat. Someone with a good ear for music would be able to distinguish one from the other

5–6. Pistol holster, with pocket for spare clip of 30 rounds — 7. Soldier, wearing German 1916-pattern steel helmet — 8–9. Bosnian infantrymen — 10. Steyr pistol, 1907-pattern, 8-mm — 11. Steyr pistol, Mark M12, 9-mm — 12. Pick and shovel
Badges of Rank:
13. Private soldier — 14. Lance-corporal — 15. Corporal — 15. Sergeant — 17. Sergeant-major — 18. Acting Second Lieutenant (no actual British equivalent) — 19 Second Lieutenant — 20. Lieutenant — 21. Captain — 22. Major — 23. Lieutenant-Colonel — 24. Colonel — 25. Major-General — 26. Lieutenant-General — 27. General — 28. Field Marshal — 29. Officer's rank star

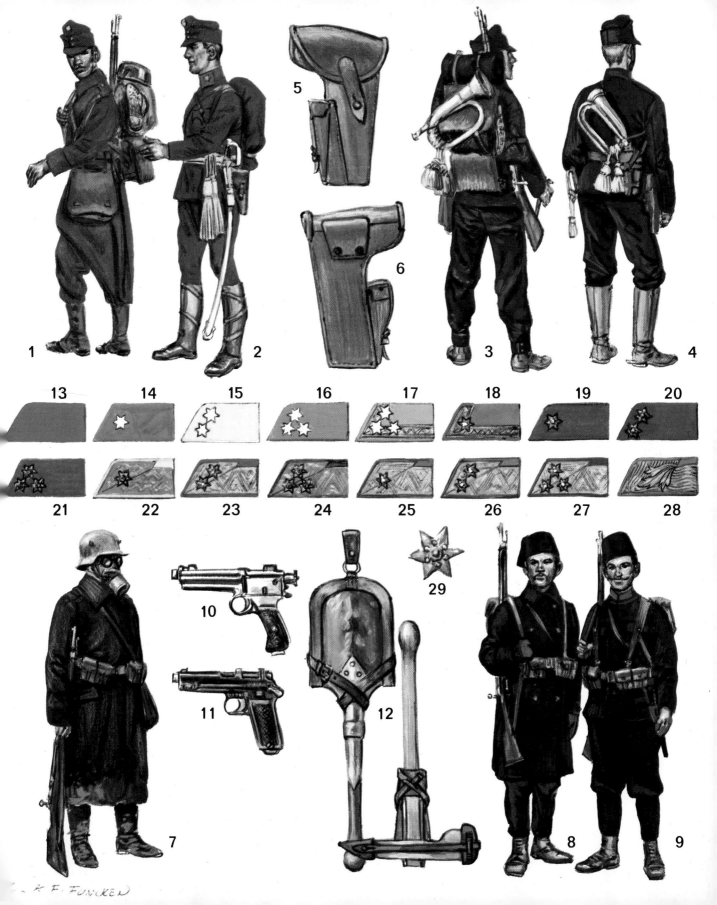

AUSTRIA AT WAR

From the beginning of the century, The Archduke Franz Ferdinand had been striving to bring the Austro-Hungarian Army up to the standard of his ideal, the German Army. He had very wisely chosen a first class officer as his Chief of Staff, Franz Conrad von Hötzendorf. Germany's proposed role for Austria in any future European war was clearly defined: to hold up any Russian offensive while Germany dealt with France.

The assassination of The Archduke, on Sunday 28 June 1914, was the spark that set off a chain-reaction, dragging in one by one the allies and the opponents of Serbia. Egged on by Berlin, the aged Emperor Franz Joseph III let himself believe that the crime had been engineered by Serbia. A settlement might have been reached if the Austrian Ambassador, Giesl, had not acted so precipitately, being convinced that a punitive expedition against Serbia would make no difference to the rest of Europe. Austria declared war on Serbia on 28 July; Germany declared war on Russia on 1 August and on France on 3 August and, on the following day, Great Britain declared war on Germany in consequence of the last's having invaded Belgium.

Austria mobilised on the night of 30–31 August, not only to attack Serbia, but also to withstand the Russians who had already mobilised their fleet, as if by chance, four days before the delivery of the Austrian ultimatum to Serbia. 'Pan-Slavism' led by Russia and 'Pan-Germanism' led by Germany had cast the die.

The Austro-Hungarian plans were in two stages: first, to destroy the Serbian Army and secondly, to attack in full strength the Russian forces in Galicia.

On 12 August 1914, the Austrians threw about twelve divisions against Serbia on the line of the River Save, but had to fall back after eight days of fierce fighting. They renewed the attack at the beginning of September and, after two months fighting, managed to take Belgrade. In the mean-time, four other Austrian armies had met with varying success against the Russians, but had finally been forced to retreat back to the heights of the Carpathians. The Serbs consolidated their forces and they launched a vigourous counter-attack on 3 December. On 13 December, the Austrians were driven out of the territory they had taken.

In 1915, the imminent entry of Italy into the War on the side of the Allies made things even more difficult for Austria-Hungary, now faced with having to fight on three fronts. Bulgaria now came in on the side of the Central Powers, which gave some hope of finishing off Serbia. Attacked on three sides by the Austrians, the Germans and the Bulgars, the Serbian army had to fall back. It only escaped destruction by undertaking a retreat, the fame of which has lived on.

Romania declared war on Austria in 1916 and proceeded to invade Transylvania, but this never constituted a serious threat. The years 1917 and 1918 proved decisive, for they showed Austria the absolute futility of continuing the struggle. On 29 October 1918, Austria asked for an armistice and this was given on 3 November. The Treaty of St Germain, in 1919, dismembered the Austro-Hungarian Empire and left Austria with a population of only 5,500,000 compared to the former Empire's 50,000,000. The casualties in the war had been over 1,200,000 dead.

AUSTRIAN MOUNTAIN INFANTRY

1–2. Mountain regiment (1917–18) — 3–4. Corporal and lance-corporal, machine-gun numbers, *Tirailleurs*. The machine gun weighed over 48-lb, and the tripod almost 40-lb — 5–6. Militiamen (1915–16) — 7. Schwarzlose machine gun, M07-12-pattern, 8 mm — 8. Mannlicher magazine rifle, M 95-pattern — 9. Magazine carbine, M 95-pattern

The Turkish Infantry

When Turkey entered the war on the side of the Central Powers, her army had already been fighting, almost uninterruptedly, for several years. In 1911, Italy had demanded the cession of the Port of Tripoli in Lybia and of Cyrenaica; in the ensuing struggle, Italy had come out on top. In 1912, faced with a Balkan Alliance between Bulgaria, Greece and Serbia, Turkey had been compelled to take up arms again in what was known as the First Balkan War. The Ottoman Empire, now in full decline, turned naturally towards Germany and, on 2 August 1914, a secret treaty of alliance was signed.

For some years past, the Turkish army had had recourse to British, French and German instructors to reorganise it on European lines. From 1909, Germany had only undertaken this thankless task with an ulterior motive that was obvious to all. The result was that the army uniform was completely Prussian in appearance when Turkey entered the war, with the exception of the traditional Turkish head-dress, the fez. However by 1909, the Turks had already adopted khaki as the colour of their service dress, though the actual hue ranged from beige to brown. The helmet worn on service had no peak, since their religion forbade them to protect their eyes from the sun.

The officers' badges of rank were worn on the shoulder, in the same way as those of the German army. The non-commissioned officers had a red edge to the shoulder-strap in the infantry and a blue one in the machine gunners.

The arms, both rifles and machine-guns, and the equipment were supplied by the Germans. The first rifle was a Mauser 1890-pattern, ·302 in but at the outbreak of hostilities a Mauser, ·312 in, was introduced.

The liability for military service started at twenty years of age, three years being spent with the colours. This was followed by six years in the reserve, nine years in the second reserve and two years in the local militia.

Russia declared war on Turkey on 4 November 1914 and on the following day, Great Britain and France did the same. At once, Turkey found herself compelled to fight on several fronts at the same time: the Suez Canal, the Caucasus, Mesopotamia and, in 1915, the Dardanelles. The initial operations in the Caucasus were decided upon by the Commander-in-Chief, Enver Pasha, who was keen to come to grips with his traditional enemies, the Russians. Disregarding the counsels of discretion of the Germans and after having halted a Russian offensive with six divisions, he advanced into the mountains with two army corps. After some success, the ill-equipped Turks were forced back on to the defensive by heavy enemy counter-attacks and, after a week of desperate fighting, Enver Pasha started to retreat. However the weather was against him and, in those early days of 1915, snow and ice made the mountains well-nigh impassable. Frozen and constantly being ambushed, the Turkish 9th Army was eventually annihilated. With the help of the Armenians who had risen in revolt against their Turkish oppressors, the Russians accounted for nearly 40,000 Turkish soldiers.

TURKISH INFANTRY: FULL DRESS

1. Officer, Infantry of the Line — 2. Non-commissioned officer, Infantry of the Line — 3–4. *Chasseurs à pied* — 5. Officer, 1st Foot Guards — 6. Drummer, 1st Foot Guards — 7. Sultan's Body Guard — 8. Officer, 1st Foot Guards, guard order — 9. Zouave of the Guard

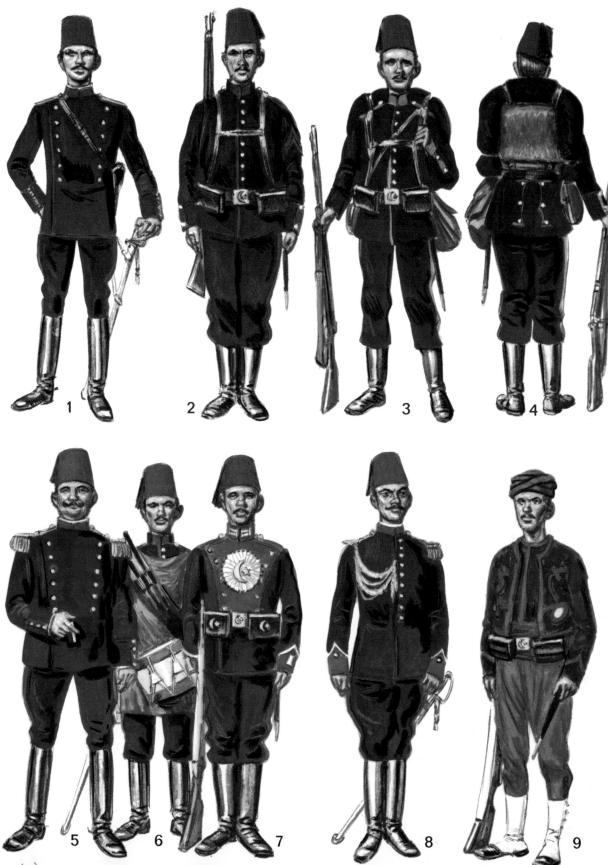

In the summer, a large-scale counter-offensive under Abdul Karim Pasha drove the Russians back but again, assisted by the Armenians, they returned to the attack and, making use of local knowledge of the tracks through the mountains, they took the Turks from the rear and defeated them once more.

Smarting under this second defeat, the Turkish Government decided to punish the Armenian traitors. The Armenian population living in Turkish territory was rounded up and deported from the combat zones, to be marched in endless columns towards Mesopotamia. The trek lasted two years and, as a result of systematic extermination, 500,000 unhappy Armenians perished. However, the Allies did nothing to punish those responsible after the war.

During the summer of 1915, the Turkish Army was increased to fifty-two divisions, totalling some 800,000 men. In April 1915, the British and the French had attempted to force the passage of the Dardanelles by making a landing on the Gallipoli Peninsula, but they came up against fierce resistance from a force of 200,000 under the Inspector General of the Turkish Army, the German General Liman von Sanders. In January 1916, the Allies were forced to withdraw to their ships. The Allied position in the Middle East was no better. The British had marched on Baghdad, but had been defeated by the Turks under German leadership. At Kut al-Imara, General Charles Townshend had been forced to surrender.

A further Russian offensive in 1916 was likewise halted. The British, on the other hand, renewed their assault on Mesopotamia, helped by the Arabs from the Hedjaz stirred up by the famous Colonel Lawrence.

In March 1917, Baghdad fell and Jerusalem followed in December. The collapse of Russia and the separate peace brought only a temporary relief to Turkey's difficulties. The British offensive in Palestine in September and October 1918, drove the Turks into retreat and an armistice was signed on 30 October. The Turks, as well as suffering the humiliation of a defeat, had lost 400,000 killed.

The Ottoman Empire was soon to collapse and to give place to the modern republic, thanks to the prodigious efforts of Mustafa Kemal, nicknamed *Atatürk* which means Father of the Turks.

TURKISH INFANTRY: SERVICE DRESS

1–4. Foot soldiers — 5, 7, 8. Officers — 6. General Officer (distinguished by the red stripe on the breeches)

The Bulgarian Infantry

In 1914, Bulgaria had come out of the Second Balkan War with the loss of some of her territory to the Greek, Romanian and Serbian Alliance, but had gained a footing on the Aegean Sea. Seizing the opportunity of profiting from the natural rancour of the defeated, Germany managed to turn Bulgaria against her Russian protectors and made the country a substantial financial loan. When the Great War broke out, the opposition from the Bulgarian neutral faction was brushed aside by the pro-German faction who were convinced that Germany would win the war. This faction was led by King Ferdinand, naturally a germanophile, since he was the son of Prince Augustus of Saxe-Coburg-Gotha. The most outspoke opponent of the royal policy, Alexander Stambolijski, was accused of *lèse-majesté* and condemned to imprisonment for life.

Having silenced the malcontents, the King ordered general mobilisation. An ultimatum from Russia did not dissuade Bulgaria from declaring war on her special enemy, Serbia, on 12 October 1915 which, not unnaturally, resulted in declarations of war by Serbia, France, Italy and Great Britain.

At war strength, the Bulgarian army numbered 400,000 men. Compulsory military service started at the age of twenty and, including reserve liability, lasted for twenty-four years. The infantry had an excellent reputation for steadiness under fire. Fighting under German command, Bulgaria took part in the offensive of the Central Powers against Serbia on 15 October 1915.

Some of the infantry wore an out-of-date brownish uniform, and some wore one of greenish grey. Ruined by the Balkan Wars, Bulgaria was nearly bankrupt and numerous uniforms received from Germany were worn during the Great War, differentiated only by some national badge. The rough canvas leggings wrapped round the legs with criss-crossed straps lent a peasant air to the costume, but hardly contributed to a smart appearance. Most of the rifles were Austrian Mannlichers.

A French attempt to come to the assistance of the Serbs was driven off by the Bulgars, the French had to fall back on Salonika. However, as the months went by, the faction in favour of neutrality returned to the field, much increased in numbers. Short of war material and wearied by the long-drawn-out trench warfare, the army started to succumb to the disastrous effects of peace propaganda. Moreover, ill-fed and dirty, the men in the trenches on the Macedonian Front fell prey to malaria.

It was in this condition that the Bulgarian Army had to face an offensive launched by the French General Louis Franchet d'Esperey on 14 September 1918. For three days they held out, fighting desperately, then the line broke and the men fled, cursing the government that had deceived them for so long and brought them misery.

BULGARIAN INFANTRY I

1–2. Reservists (note their out-of-date rifles) — 3–4. Drummers, wearing comforter — 5. Foot soldier, in full marching order, winter dress — 6. Officer — 7. Bugler (1908) — 8. Warrant Officer (1908) (the rank is indicated by the lace on the collar and cuffs and by the shoulder-straps: the chevrons on the left arm denote length of service) — 9. Officer, wearing comforter

1   2   3   4

5   6   7   8   9

L. & F. Funcken

King Ferdinand, who was no longer under any delusions concerning the Second Reich, hastened to release Stambolijski to the mutineers, in order to persuade them not to march on the capital. On 29 September 1918, Bulgaria capitulated; after calling in vain upon President Wilson of the United States to come to her help. King Ferdinand abdicated in favour of his son, Boris, on 4 October 1918 and sought refuge at Coburg in Germany.

Germany saw her own collapse foreshadowed in Bulgaria's and realised that it was imperative that she should seek a negotiated peace as soon as possible.

A year later, the Treaty of Neuilly deprived Bulgaria of her territories in Thrace and in Macedonia, including access to the Aegean Sea. In addition to enormous economic difficulties, she now found herself faced with the problem of supporting 250,000 Bulgarian refugees thrown out by the new owners of the land she had lost. Perhaps even worse, were her casualties: out of an army of 1,200,000, 100,000 had been killed.

BULGARIAN INFANTRY II

1. Foot soldier (1908) — 2–3. Foot soldiers, summer and winter dress — 4. Foot Guards (1908) — 5. Reserve Officer — 6. Reservists

PART THREE

ARMOUR AND AIRCRAFT

Tanks and Armoured Cars

In the early stages, the Great War of 1914–1918 had, like any other, been a war of movement, often rapid movement, but after the Marne, things had suddenly come to a halt. We have already noticed the efforts that were made to break the deadlock and the catastrophic results of trying to take an entrenched position by frontal attack. Attempts had been made to reduce the losses that such attacks involved and much thought had been given to the matter. The only solution appeared to be to provide some sort of a shield as was used in the Middle Ages, either an individual or a collective shield, the latter on wheels, behind which one might hope to reach the enemy's positions unscathed. However, most such experiments were quickly abandoned, as they were too vulnerable to artillery fire.

Armoured cars carrying machine-guns had been in use since the beginning of the War and they had proved effective against both cavalry and infantry in mobile warfare on many occasions. They were ineffective however in trench warfare for they could not cross the cratered ground.

The Birth of the Tank

The credit for the invention of the tank cannot be given to any one person. With the advance of scientific awareness, the thinking man applied his new knowledge to the solving of everyday problems and crossing broken ground was one that confronted the large-scale agriculturist as well as the soldier, although the conditions under which this had to be done were very different. In the United States of America, the Holt Caterpillar

Tractor had been developed for agricultural purposes, and the military potentialities of this had not gone unnoticed.

In 1912, an Australian, L. E. de Mole, had submitted to the British War Office a design for a military vehicle that was strikingly similar to the tank that was actually produced in 1916; but Mr de Mole was in advance of his time and his brilliant invention got no further than the pigeon-holes of the War Office.

The name 'Tank' was chosen as a cover-name from several other suggestions, as being reasonably descriptive of the shape yet sufficiently non-committal. In the official correspondence and discussions that led to its creation, the term 'Land Ship' was used but this could hardly have failed to excite curiosity. So the name has remained: Tank Corps, later Royal Tank Corps and finally Royal Tank Regiment.

Several people have laid claim to having invented the tank, but the machines that went into action for the first time at the Battle of Flers-Courcelette on 15 September 1916, were really the product of the combined efforts, in the face of considerable opposition, of a handful of Naval and Army Officers and Naval and Civil Engineers. The tank was probably properly conceived at a discussion in October 1914 between Lieutenant-

BRITISH TANKS I

1. Mark I (male) (1916) — 2. Mark I (female) (1917) —
3. Mark IV (1917)

Colonel E. D. Swinton, Royal Engineers, Captain T. G. Tulloch, Royal Artillery and Lieutenant-Colonel M. P. A. Hankey, Royal Marines, Secretary of the Committee of Imperial Defence.

The credit for the ultimate production of the tank undoubtedly goes to Colonel Swinton, Commodore Murray Sueter, Royal Naval Air Service, and Mr Winston Churchill, First Lord of the Admiralty, for their pertinacity and foresight.

As we have mentioned, once static warfare was established, frontal attacks were doomed to failure. The narrow strip between the two lines of trenches, known as No-Man's Land, was filled with barbed wire entanglements and it had been found that prolonged artillery bombardment had little effect in breaking this up, whilst making the ground even more difficult to cross. Moreover, it disclosed the intended point of attack. What was needed, therefore, was some means of making a gap through which the infantry could pass, at the same time preserving the element of surprise.

Various ideas were propounded, vehicles with wheels 40 feet in diameter, vehicles with pedrails (hinged pads fitted to the rim of the wheel), variations on the steam-roller, vehicles that could lay a bridge in front of them and pick it up again after they had crossed it and, of course, caterpillar tractors. The final requirement decided upon was that the vehicle to be tried out must be able to cross an 8 ft gap without climbing and climb a 5 ft parapet. If possible, it was to have a speed of 4 mph. The armour was to be 8 mm at the sides and 6 mm on top. Originally, the idea had been to arm it either with a 2 pounder gun or a 2·95 in Q.F. mountain gun, but the former was considered too light and it was doubtful whether there were enough of the latter available. So, a naval 6 pounder gun was decided upon instead. The crew was to be eight men and a tracked vehicle was decided upon.

The original idea had been to have a tracked chassis carrying a body. Then Lieutenant W. G. Wilson, Royal Naval Volunteer Reserve, hit upon the idea of passing the tracks round the body. The difficulty that these got in the way of all-round fire was solved by placing the armament in sponsons at each side of the hull.

On 29 January 1916, a preliminary trial was held with two tanks: 'Little Willie' which had a tracked chassis and 'Big Willie' which incorporated Lieutenant Wilson's modification of the tracks running round the body. This was attended by most of those who had been concerned with the development of the tank since 1914. 'Big Willie' had an overall length of 31 ft 3 in, a width of 8 ft 3 in, with a sponson of 13 ft 8 in, and a height of 8 ft. The total weight, with ammunition and a crew of eight men, was 28 tons 8 cwt.

'Then the trial began. First, the tank tackled the "official test" of climbing a parapet 4 feet 6 inches high and crossing a trench 5 feet wide. Then came an "active service test", in which it crawled into a prepared dug-out shelter, climbed out and over a "British" trench, crossed two shell craters 12 feet wide and 6 feet deep, went through a stream with marshy edges, climbed the slope beyond and pushed through a "German" wire entanglement, then over the trench beyond, turned round behind this and back to the stream, passed down the marshy bed, and surmounted a double breastwork 5 feet 6 inches high–despite the handicap of approaching it in the mud.'[40]

In view of the tank's success in this first trial, it was felt justifiable to ask the Secretary of State for

[40] *The Tanks: The History of the Royal Tank Regiment and its predecessors . . .* by B. H. Liddell Hart. Volume I.

BRITISH TANKS II, AND ARMOURED CARS

1. Mark V (male) (1918) — 2. Whippet medium tank (1918) — 3. Lanchester armoured car, Royal Naval Air Service (1914) — 4. Delaunay-Belleville armoured car, Royal Naval Air Service (1915) — 5. Austin armoured car (the most widely-used on all fronts) — 6. Tank crew, wearing anti-splinter mask (the impact of bullets on the outside of the hull of the tank caused very dangerous splintering within)

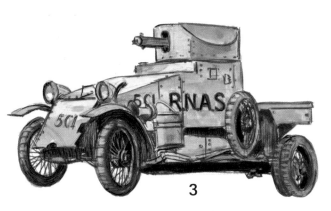

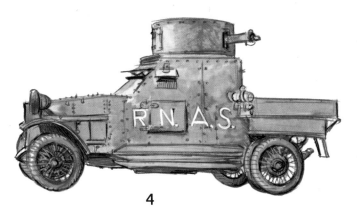

3

4

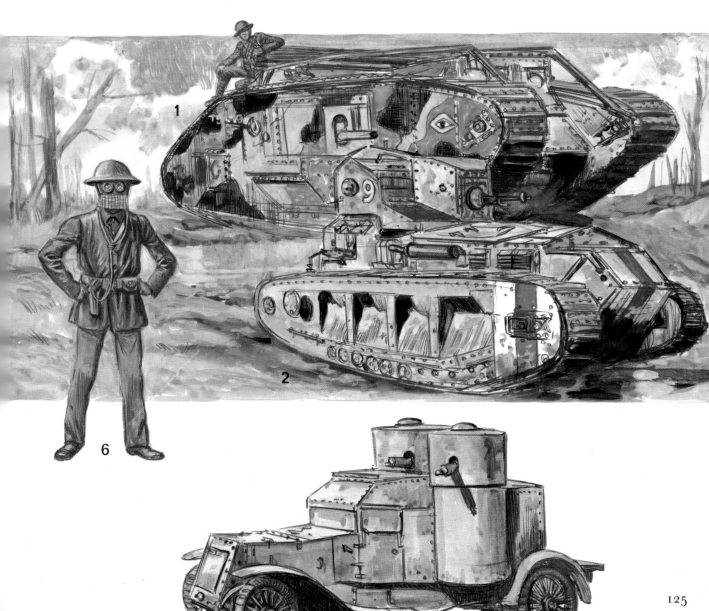

1

6

2

5

L. & F. FUNCKEN.

125

War, Lord Kitchener, to witness a further trial on 2 February. When that day came, 'Big Willie' made its debut before the great. All went well but, notwithstanding, Kitchener was far from enthusiastic and remarked that it was a 'pretty mechanical toy' that would be 'very quickly knocked out by the enemy's artillery'.

On 8 February 1916, King George V came to witness a 'command performance' arranged at short notice, went for a ride in 'Big Willie' and said that he considered that the Army should have a large number. This tipped the balance and by the end of the month, approval had been given for 100 tanks to be ordered. At the same time as production of the tank was started, the training of volunteers to fight them began.

BRITISH ARMOUR

The first tanks were known as Mark I and, according to their armament, were known as 'male' or 'female'. The female tank, armed with machine-guns, was intended to support the male tank, armed with guns, which would carry out the main task according to the tactics conceived by Swinton.

A male tank weighed 30 tons, had a speed of just over $3\frac{1}{2}$ mph, and a range of about 12 miles. It was just over 26 ft long, about 14 ft wide, and 8 ft high. This tank could be fought with a crew of four, but the full complement was an officer and seven men: the tank commander, a driver, four gunners and two mechanics.

The male tank carried two 6 pounder guns and four Hotchkiss machine-guns, and the female tank had one Hotchkiss and four Vickers machine-guns. The Mark I tank had a periscope with glass prisms which proved dangerous. They were quickly replaced by metal mirrors. The crew had to endure the uproar of the six-cylinder Daimler engine set in the middle of the tank where it gave off highly unpleasant fumes as well as great heat.

The total secrecy that had protected the creation of this new arm had resulted in its being given a number of titles, such as Tank Detachment and Armoured Car Section of the Motor Machine-gun Service, neither of which was as innocent as one would have hoped. Finally the name Heavy Branch, Machine-gun Corps was adopted. All the same, the enemy never tumbled to what was happening. In July 1917, the Heavy Branch of the M.G.C. was reconstituted as the Tank Corps.

The original Heavy Branch consisted of 184 Officers and 1,610 other ranks. The tactical unit was the company, composed of four sections each of six tanks (three male and three female) with one in reserve. There were six companies, each designated by a letter of the alphabet. It is from this that the mistake has arisen of terming the Mark I tank the 'Crème de Menthe'. In fact, each tank in 'C' Company had been given a name of a French wine or liqueur by the crew, and each commenced with the letter C: Champagne, Cognac, Chablis, Chartreuse, Cordon Rouge.

Colonel Swinton was not, however, destined to lead the first attack by the monsters that he had conceived. He had to content himself with raising and training the new units as he had too little battle experience to fight with them. The honour of going into action for the first time fell to C and D Companies, who attacked on the Somme at dawn on 15 September 1916. Their objective was an enemy position, established in depth with numerous nests of machine-guns. The tanks led the attack, followed by the infantry of three British Army Corps. Out of 49 tanks, only 32 reached the start line, the remainder having broken down, bogged down or lost themselves in the dark. With other break-downs and tanks getting stuck in shell-holes, only 18 tanks actually took part in the final assault. The psychological effect on the

FRENCH TANKS I

1–2. Saint-Chamond — 3. Schneider

Germans was unbelievable. There was panic in the trenches when the tanks appeared.

The tank 'Crème de Menthe' gained its fame that day at Courcelette, when it made a successful attack on a sugar factory that had been made a strong point. Other tanks, less fortunate or more venturesome, were captured but the day had been a success and the effect on the enemy's morale very considerable.

The success of this first action resulted in the press indulging in a frenzy of exaggeration, asserting that Germany would be brought to her knees in a matter of weeks. The War Office ignored this hysteria but raised an additional eight companies for service in France and re-organised the whole into four battalions, while the number of companies in Britain was increased from two to five. A battalion now consisted of three companies, each of four sections of five tanks, together with a reserve section. At the beginning of 1917, the establishment was modified and a company was reduced to three sections each of four tanks.

The lessons of the war led the engineers to improve the original tank notably in removing the stabilising wheels in rear, which were particularly vulnerable to artillery fire. Small numbers of Mark II and Mark III tanks appeared and these were, generally speaking, like the Mark I. The Mark IV tank included a number of improvements, particularly in the armour, since the Germans had developed an anti-tank bullet (Type K); every rifleman carried five rounds of it and it could also be fired by the machine-gun.

The last model was the Mark V tank, which appeared in July 1918 but, like its predecessors, it was heavy and difficult to manoeuvre. Another type of tank had been developed in the United Kingdom in November 1916, the Tritton Chaser, officially known as the Medium A but generally called a Whippet, after the racing dog. This tank weighed only 14 tons and had a speed of 8 mph. There was a crew of three and it carried four machine-guns. The Whippet first saw action at Colincamps in March 1918, where it proved itself and, strangely, was thought by the Germans to be one of theirs. The Whippet was also engaged at Frémincourt and at Amiens in 1918, but there were never more than 200 in service.

FRENCH ARMOUR

In France, Colonel (later General) Jean-Baptiste Estienne had pursued a similar line to Colonel Swinton, and two types of armoured fighting vehicle had been evolved, the Schneider and the Saint-Chamond. Both were armed with the famous 'French 75' gun, the first with two machine-guns in addition and the second with four.

The Schneider weighed $13\frac{1}{2}$ tons and had a crew of seven. It had a maximum speed of 5 mph, and was fitted with a beak designed to break through the barbed wire, which earned it the nickname of Rhinoceros. The Saint-Chamond, which weighed 23 tons, had the same maximum speed and carried a crew of nine. The first French tanks made their appearance in the same month as the British.

A number of serious defects were soon found and, badly employed militarily, the French

FRENCH TANKS II

1. Section through a Renault tank — 2. Renault tank, F.T. 17, with octagonal turret mounted with machine gun — 3. Renault tank, with rounded turret mounted with 37 mm gun, off-set at an angle of 45° to the left — 4. Renault tank 1st U.S. Tank Brigade (1918) with turret off-set 45° to the right — 5. French tank crew — 6. Arm badge, 301st U.S. Tank Battalion — 7. Arm badge, U.S. Tank Corps — 8. Badge, French Tank Corps (*Artillerie d'assaut*)

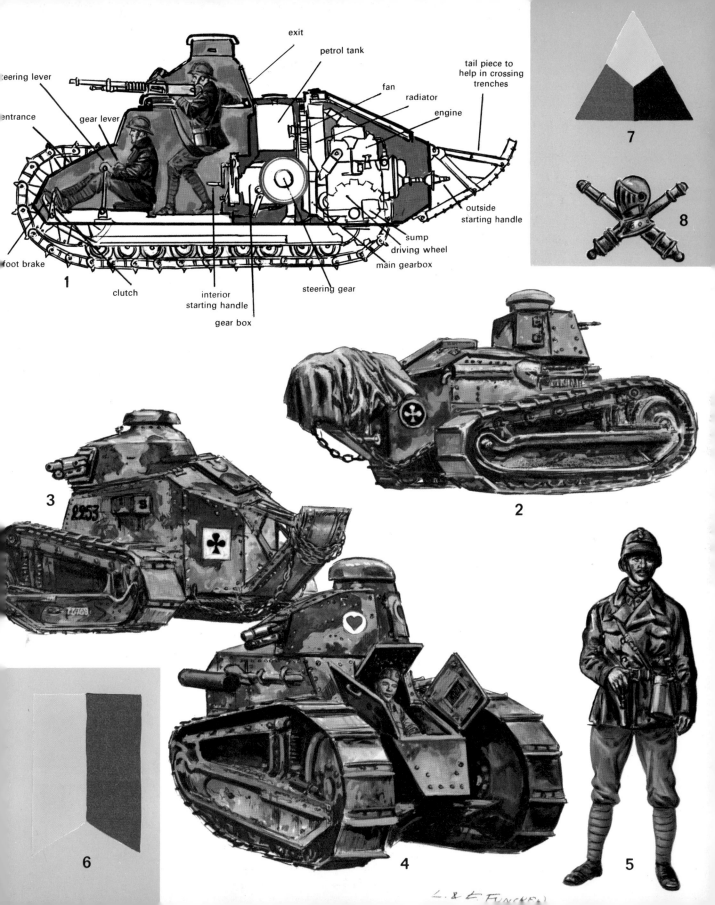

1

steering lever

entrance

gear lever

exit

petrol tank

fan

radiator

engine

tail piece to help in crossing trenches

outside starting handle

sump

driving wheel

main gearbox

steering gear

foot brake

clutch

interior starting handle

gear box

2

3

2253

4

5

6

7

8

L. & E. FUNCKEN

tank did not enjoy the success of the British. It was decided not to develop the two original types but to break fresh ground, as a new design had been conceived by Colonel Estienne and Monsieur Louis Renault. The Renault light tank became one of the most famous tanks of the First World War. In 1918, the French Army had a holding of 3,000. This remarkable machine was the forerunner of the modern armoured fighting vehicle, the four-cylinder engine was at the back and the tank which weighed $6\frac{3}{4}$ tons, had a speed of just over 5 mph and a range of 25 miles. There was a crew of two, a gunner in command and a driver. The turret had an all-round traverse and could carry a 37 mm gun or a Hotchkiss machine-gun.

The French armour was officially styled Special Artillery, though it also acquired a number of nicknames.

GERMAN ARMOUR

The Germans were slow to adopt the new arm and contented themselves with using captured tanks. However on 21 March 1918, the formidable 'Sturmpanzerwagen A7V' (Armoured assault vehicle) made its appearance. It weighed 32 tons, was 24 ft long, 10 ft wide and more than 10 ft high.

This enormous tank carried a crew of eighteen, but an even larger one, the 'K-Wagen', which had been planned for 1919, was to have had a crew of 22, to have been powered by two 650 C.V. engines and armed with four 77 mm guns and ten machine-guns.

There was a considerable disparity between the armour on the two sides and a German expert says, bitterly, that there were 6,000 Allied tanks against 20 German at the end of the war.

GERMAN TANKS AND ARMOURED CARS

1. Section through A7V tank — 2. A7V tank — 3. Tank badge, worn on left breast pocket — 4. Büssing armoured car (1915) — 5. Mannesmann-Mulag armoured car

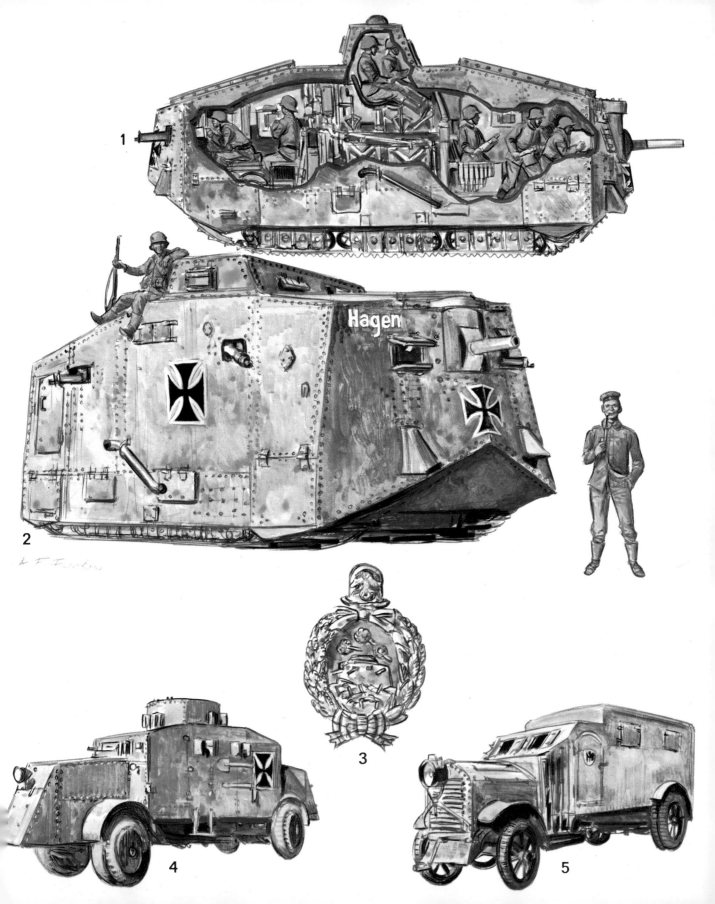

1

2

Hagen

3

4

5

The Air Forces

Following the sensational demonstration by the pioneer American aviator, Wilbur Wright, in Paris in 1908, a new era opened for aviation in Europe. In 1909, Blériot crossed the Channel in 32 minutes and the aeroplane began to be taken seriously. The French aircraft industry expanded quickly, and its reputation was such that the air forces of most other countries had French equipment. Germany alone stood aloof and developed her own aircraft industry.

Many military historians would have it that it was not until the Great War that the aeroplane was used as a weapon of war. In fact aircraft were used by the Italians in their operations in Tripolitania in 1911 and, in the Balkan War of 1912–13, the Bulgarians made the first aerial bombardment when they attacked the Turkish positions about Adrianople[41].

The following is an analysis:

HF 1, 7, 13, 19	manufactured by Henri Farman
MF 2, 5, 8, 16, 20	manufactured by Maurice Farman
BL 3, 9, 10, 18	manufactured by Blériot
D 4, 6	manufactured by Deperdussin
C 11, 25	manufactured by Caudron
N 12	manufactured by Nieuport
V 14, 21, 24	manufactured by Voisin
B 17	manufactured by Bréguet
REP 15	manufactured by Robert-Emmanuel Pelleterie
DO 22	manufactured by Dorand-Anzani
MS 23	manufactured by Morane-Saulnier
BLC three cavalry	manufactured by Blériot

THE ALLIED AIR FORCES

The French Air Force

At the outbreak of the Great War, the French air arm was considered the best, even by Germany. However it was only a part of the Engineers and its role was limited to reconnaissance and observation. In August 1914, there were twenty-one squadrons for general duty and three specially allocated to the cavalry. Each squadron consisted of eight aircraft and each was designated by the squadron number with initials indicating the make of aircraft flown. Upon mobilisation four additional squadrons, Nos 22 to 25, were raised.

41 The bomb used is shown on page 145, figure 10.

FRENCH AIR FORCE I

Aircraft:
1. Morane-Saulnier N — 2. Nieuport 12 — 3. Nieuport Bébé — 4. Nieuport 17 — 5. Nieuport 21bis — 6. Nieuport 28, in U.S. service — 7. Farman HF-7 — 8. Caudron C-4 — 9. Spad 13, in U.S. service
Pilots' and etc badges:
10. Pilot — 11. Pilot under instruction — 17. Airship pilot — 18. Observer — 19. Air crew
Arm badges:
12. Mechanic — 13. Engineer — 14. Non-commissioned officer, flying branch — 15. Officer, flying branch
Collar badge:
16. Officer, flying corps
Miscellaneous:
20. Engineer (1915) — 21. Mechanic, working dress (1915)

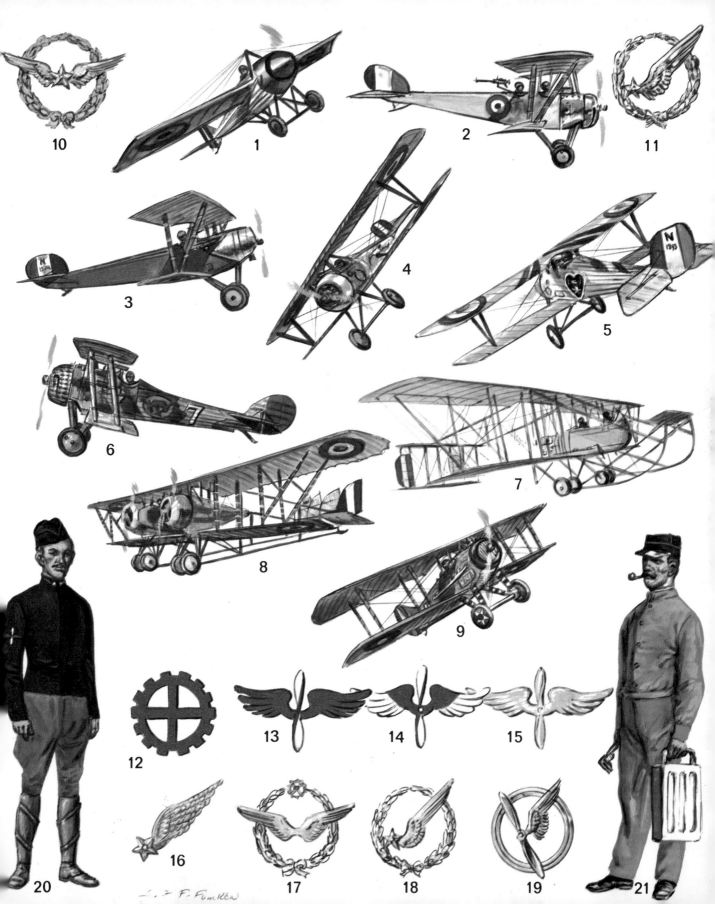

10

1

2

11

3

4

5

6

7

8

9

12

13

14

15

16

17

18

19

20

21

F. Funcken

The first pilots were recruited from specially selected officers and non-commissioned officers who had taken an interest in flying, and were drawn from all arms of the service. Whereas the airship and balloon service wore a uniform like that of the engineers, the pilots paraded in every uniform known in the French Army. When horizon blue was introduced in 1915, the pilots and observers often continued to wear the old uniform which distinguished them from the ground staff. The flying kit, at the beginning of the War, was very varied and included civilian items. Only the helmet and suit were issue.

In 1914, the airship and balloon service consisted of seven large airships, and one section of captive balloons per army corps[42].

The British Air Forces

The Royal Flying Corps, raised in 1912, consisted of a Naval Wing and a Military Wing. The Naval Wing, known as the Royal Naval Air Service[43], had an aeroplane section and an airship section. The Military Wing, known as the Royal Flying Corps, had a squadron of airships and kites and, originally, seven squadrons of aeroplanes.

At the outbreak of the War, the RNAS had 93 aircraft and the RFC 179 aircraft. The original aircraft were of French manufacture, but these were eventually replaced by ones of British manufacture such as the De Havilland, the Avro and the Bristol, and various types made at the Royal Aircraft Factory.

The Belgian Air Force

The tiny Belgian Air Force consisted, in 1914, of sixteen H. Farman bi-planes, organised in four squadrons, together with a fifth squadron of five requisitioned French-built aircraft. It had also two captive balloons and two small training airships.

The Russian Air Force

In addition to 200 French aircraft (Farman, Voisin and Blériot), the Russians had a number of enormous four-engined aircraft, the first of their kind in the world. These had been produced by Professor Igor Sikorski and were named after the legendary hero, Ilia Mouromets. This bomber became the pride and joy of the Russian Imperial Air Service.

The Italian Air Force

The Military Air Corps, the name by which the Italian air force was known, had French Hanriot H-D1 1916 fighters, and two Italian types, the Ansaldo and the Caproni. The former was a good long-range reconnaissance aircraft and the latter was a sturdy heavy bomber.

42 See Volume II, Engineers.
43 See Volume II, Navies.

FRENCH AIR FORCE II

1. Officer, flying corps — 2. Private, 2nd Air Group — 3. Non-commissioned officer, flying corps — 4. Officer, in fur coat — 5–8. Officers, flying corps — 9. Winter flying kit
Aircraft:
10. Bréguet 14 — 11. Caudron C-23 — 12. Nieuport Tri-plane — 13. Spad 7
Weapons:
14. Browning machine gun (U.S.A.) (bottom); Hotchkiss machine gun (France) (centre); various incendiary darts and bombs, that with hooks for use against airships, and that on the left being a steel anti-personnel dart

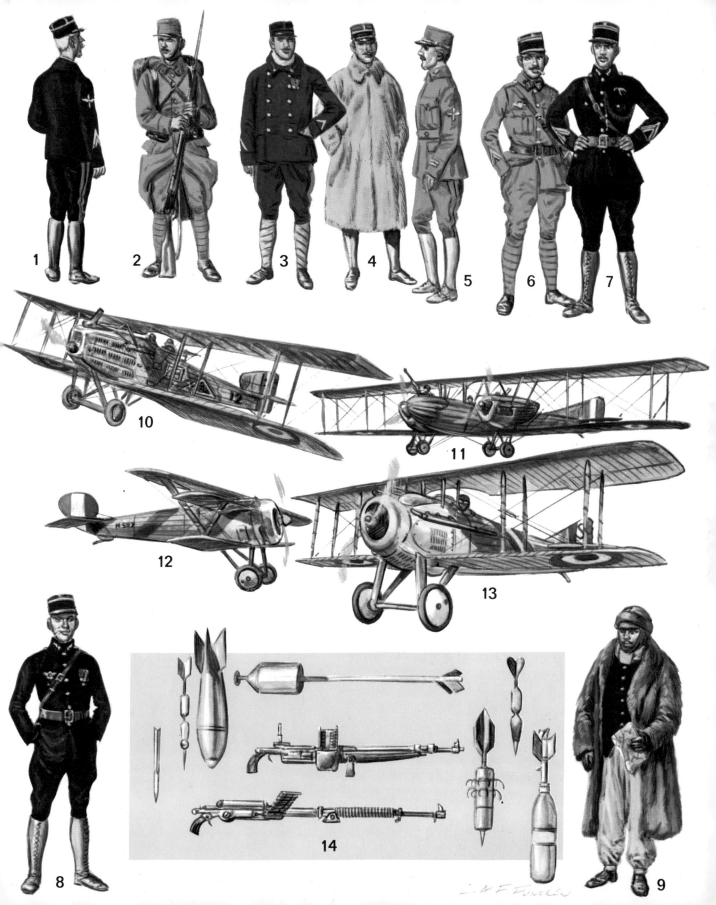

The United States Air Force

When the United States entered the War, she had no aircraft capable of taking part in aerial combat. The United States Air Service was equipped with French, British and Italian aircraft, and consisted of one fighter squadron and one reconnaissance squadron. Within three months, the strength had increased to eleven squadrons.

In fact, volunteers from the U.S.A. had been joining up in France as pilots from 1915. They received a monthly salary of 200 gold francs, paid by a committee of which W. K. Vanderbilt was president. They also received monetary rewards for decorations awarded and for victories in the air. A Legion of Honour was worth 1,500 gold francs and an aircraft shot down 250 gold francs.

Thirty-eight American volunteers served in the 1st and 2nd Lafayette Squadrons known, respectively, as N 124 and SPA 124 since one had Nieuport and the other Spad aircraft. Nine lost their lives. Later, the French formed a Lafayette Flying Corps to which all the United States volunteers were transferred and this Corps lost 65 men in the course of the War.

THE AIR FORCES OF THE CENTRAL POWERS

In 1914, the Germans had 32 squadrons each of six aircraft for general service, and 18 squadrons each of four aircraft for the defence of fortresses and the like.

Both monoplanes, known as *Taube* on account of the resemblance of their wings to those of a pigeon, and a variety of types of biplane were in service. These latter included the Albatross, the Aviatik, the L.V.G. and the D.F.W. (the last two being the initials of the manufacturing firms). The German air force also had fifteen airships, which the British called Zeppelins after the inventor, Graf Ferdinand von Zeppelin (1838–1917). These were used for terror raids, but

proved highly vulnerable. Captive balloons were used for observation[44].

Right at the beginning of the War, the Germans were fortunate in securing the services of an aircraft engineer of Dutch extraction, Anthony Fokker. His first monoplane was the Eindecker I (*eindecker* means monoplane), and this was followed by a series of quite remarkable aircraft. Fokker perfected a system whereby a machine-gun could fire between the blades of the airscrew. On more than one occasion, his inventions gave Germany undisputed air superiority. We shall refer to this again when dealing with fighters.

The Austro-Hungarian air force consisted, for the most part, of German-made aircraft but one type was manufactured in the country. It was the Lohner made by Jacob Lohner of Vienna. There were 70 aircraft, divided into nine squadrons.

The remaining countries, on both sides, had air forces of insignificant size.

---

44 See Volume II, Engineers.

GREAT BRITAIN:
THE ROYAL FLYING CORPS

Aircraft:
1. BE-12 — 2. BE-2C — 3. SE-2A — 4. SE-5A — 5. Sopwith Camel — 6. Gun Bus — 7. Bristol Scout — 8. FE-2B — 9. De Havilland — 10. Bristol F-2A
Miscellaneous:
11. Cap badge — 12. Pilot's badge — 13–14. Pilots (1914) — 15. 112 lb bomb

THE DEVELOPMENT OF FLYING

At first, the aeroplane was looked upon as a dangerous toy, but both sides quickly realised that it was of the utmost importance as an arm and great technical advances were made from 1915 on.

Air Reconnaissance

At the beginning of the War, aircraft were only able to fly at between 300 and 600 feet, because of the lack of engine power. The slower aircraft were considered the most suitable for observing enemy positions, but it was soon found that they could be brought down by rifle fire.

Artillery fire was directed by a code based on the pilot's evolutions in the air, but this could be negatived by even a slight mist. A system of rocket signals was tried but this was no more successful. Then at the beginning of 1915, the development of wireless, in particular by the British, brought great advances in air observation which were helped on by Colonel Estienne[45].

There was more to fire direction than merely saying 'A bit more to the left.' or 'A bit more to the right.' A system was evolved where the objective was taken to be the centre of a clock face, XII representing north, VI south and so on. In addition, the clock face was marked with concentric circles like a target at increasing radii of 10, 20, 30, 50, 100, 200 yards, each circle being given a letter starting at the outside. Thus 'Three o'clock, B.' would indicate that the shot had fallen 100 yards to the east of the target, and the necessary correction could then be made.

The destruction of the reconnaissance aircraft became a matter of prime importance for both sides, and aircraft seemed the most suitable means of doing it. The pistols and carbines that were used in some of the earlier aerial combats, however, were really supplied for the pilot's self-protection if he were shot down. The first aircraft to be brought down was an Austrian which was rammed by the Russian pilot Nesterov.

Another Russian pilot, Alexander Kasakov, used a balloon anchor on a rope to rip the wings of his opponent's aircraft. In the less unusual sphere, the first aerial victory with a machine-gun was achieved when it was mounted on a Voisin of the French 24th Squadron. Sergeant Frantz and Corporal Quenault brought down a German Aviatik on 5 October 1914. The corporal fired 47 single shots from his Hotchkiss light machine-gun, knowing that it had a tendency to spray if it was fired on automatic.

An earlier attempt by a British pilot named Strange to fit his aircraft with a machine-gun had been a failure because it was unable to gain sufficient height with the extra weight. With the development of more powerful aircraft, it became possible to arm them with improved types of machine-gun, notably the Hotchkiss, the Lewis, the Vickers and the Maxim.

45 See page 128.

RUSSIAN, BELGIAN, ITALIAN, AND
UNITED STATES AIR FORCES
Russia:
6. Morane — 7. Ilia-Mouromets — 9. Badge, worn on shoulder strap
Belgium:
1–2. Air crew — 5. Farman — 10. Cap badge
Italy:
8. Hanriot
United States of America:
3–4. Air crew — 11. Pilot under instruction — 12. Pilot — 13. Pilot (second pattern) — 14. Curtiss — 15. Morse — 16. Salmson
  Note. These last three aircraft were used only for training in the U.S.A.

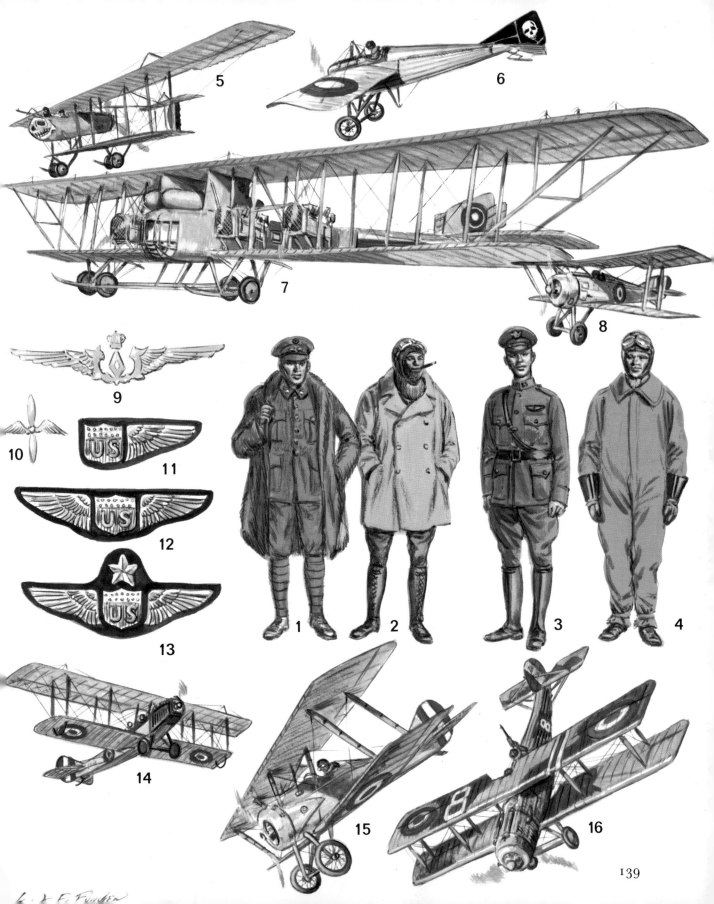

5

6

7

8

9

10

11

12

13

1

2

3

4

14

15

16

139

Fighters

The original task of the fighters was to protect the reconnaissance biplanes. The machine-gun was set at an angle in front, so that it would not hit the airscrew whilst firing. The difficulty of effectively firing a gun set in this manner need not be emphasised and the average pilot was unable to get any results.

A French pilot, Roland Garros, who had already become known as a stunt man before the War, devised a means of firing through the airscrew along the axis of the aircraft. He attached to the rear face of each blade a triangle of steel which deflected the bullets if they happened to touch the airscrew when it came between them and the target. These armoured plates were known as deflectors. The idea however had some disadvantages in practice: it increased the weight of the airscrew; it absorbed power; it bent the blades and the impact of the bullets on the deflectors was transmitted to the propeller-shaft!

It is probable, however, that the deflector was actually invented by a Frenchman named Gilbert, but that the name of Garros became attached to it as the result of the latter's brilliant exploits. At first, equipped with deflectors, Garros greatly distinguished himself by shooting down five aircraft in eight days to the consternation of the enemy. His luck was short-lived and, on 19 April 1915, as a result of engine-failure brought about by the strain of his airscrew, he came down in the enemy lines and was taken prisoner before he could destroy the deflectors. Garros was taken to Germany, but later escaped and rejoined the Cigognes squadron; he was killed in 1918. Gilbert, then working as a test pilot, was killed in the same year.

The Germans were delighted to discover how the French fighters were able to fire through the airscrew, and immediately entrusted Fokker with reproducing the device and improving upon it if possible. The Dutchman–he had not then been naturalised German–worked wonders and he prepared drawings for a far more efficient deflector within forty-eight hours. This was not attached to the blades of the airscrew but placed between the airscrew and the muzzle of the gun and operated by a cam, it was geared so that it rose when each blade came opposite the muzzle. It should be noted that this improved deflector was quite a different thing from the Fokker synchronised machine-gun, with which we shall deal later.

Even if the Fokker deflector was not perfect, it undoubtedly gave the German pilots a considerable advantage; flying over the German positions became virtually impossible. The British described it as the period of the 'Fokker scourge'. In a moment of inspiration, Fokker had also devised a triple-barrel machine-gun, working with a deflector but, fortunately for the Allies, this was considered too heavy for the aircraft.

The new situation meant that the Allies were forced to protect a single reconnaissance with a host of fighters. The British went ahead with the

BRITISH AND ITALIAN AIR FORCES AND VARIOUS WEAPONS

Great Britain:
1. Sopwith Tri-plane — 3. DH-V — 5. Handley 0/400 — 7. Kangaroo — 9. Lewis machine gun — 10. 750lb bomb — 11. Section through an anti-submarine bomb — 13. Air crew
Italy:
2. Hanriot — 4. Ansaldo — 6. Caproni — 14. Air crew
Germany:
8. Spandau machine gun
United States of America:
12. Marlin machine gun

production of aircraft with rear engines, which allowed the machine-gunner to fire unhampered and did away with the problem of firing through the airscrew. Against these advantages were set a loss of equilibrium and manœuvreability and much less power.

In France, the Garros deflector had proved a failure, more than one pilot killed himself as a result of it. The deflector had an element of Russian Roulette about it. Someone then had the idea of mounting a machine-gun on the upper plane, but this had disastrous effects on the aerodynamics and acted as a brake.

Then the tide changed. A Fokker lost its way one day and the Dutchman's secret was discovered. It was adopted at once, and the balance was restored. In the course of the summer of 1916, the legendary *Eindecker* was outclassed by the Allied fighters; the Nieuport *Bébé*, the Sopwith Pup and the Spad. Realising the importance of air-superiority, the opposing sides engaged in fiercer and fiercer air battles. After an enormous effort, the Germans regained the upper hand by introducing new types of aircraft, notably the Albatross which carried two machine-guns. This was the first heavily-armed fighter.

The year 1916 proved crucial to the German air forces, which were reorganised into a single service. On 8 October, both the air forces and the anti-aircraft organisation were placed under the command of General von Höppner. They were styled the *Luftstreitkräfte*, in effect, the German Air Force. The different squadrons were grouped into wings: fighter, escort and ground attack. Each fighter wing originally consisted of 14 aircraft, increased later to 18, though usually of only 16 aircraft.

By January 1917, the German Air Force had 48 reconnaissance squadrons, 30 escort squadrons, 30 fighter squadrons and 93 air observation post squadrons, together with three squadrons of twin-engined Gotha bombers totalling about a hundred aircraft. The reorganisation of the German Air Force and the introduction of the Albatross once again put the Allies in a very difficult position. The British suffered particularly heavy losses, especially in April 1917.

A further advance was made by the Germans when they formed fighter groups, of which No 1 (4, 6, 10 and 11 wings) was commanded by the famous fighter pilot Manfred Freiherr von Richthofen, the Red Baron. The whole formation was concentrated behind the lines and could be brought up by rail to any threatened area. The scheme was so successful that three more groups were raised.

In imitation of the French pilot Navarre who had flown an extraordinary aircraft painted red over Verdun in 1916, Richthofen chose the same colour and painted all the aircraft under his command in that colour, so that his pilots could recognise each other easily. The Germans took to painting their aircraft in such fantastic colours that these itinerant squadrons, travelling by train with all their bags and baggage, became known as the 'Circus'.

GERMAN AIR FORCE I

1. Albatross 'Taube' (1914) — 2. Fokker Eindecker IV (1915) — 3. Fokker E-III (1915) — 4. Aviatik D-1 (1917) (Austrian) — 5. Rumpler C-1 (1915) — 6. Albatross C-1 (1915) — 6a. Detail of 6, showing sleeve through fuselage enabling gunner to have all-round field of fire — 7. Airship, commonly known as a Zeppelin — 8–9. Observation and bombing cars, which the Zeppelins could let down on cables 1,000 to 1,500 yards long, thereby allowing the airship to remain unseen above the cloud-ceiling
A Landing Ground at Night (bottom):
  A. Wind-vane controlling the lighting of the red lights showing the cardinal points of the compass;
  B. White light showing centre of landing ground;
  C, D, E, F. The cardinal points;
  G. Light flashing the code for the landing ground.

1

2

3

7

4

5

6

6a

8

9

C

A

G

B

D

E

F

In the meantime, Fokker had given further consideration to the question of firing through the airscrew and had devised the first synchronised machine-gun. With the introduction of armour-piercing bullets, the deflector no longer worked. The synchronised machine-gun worked on the same principle as the deflector but the cam, instead of raising and lowering the deflector, operated the mechanism of the gun which only fired when no blade was in the way.

Fokker's new invention boded ill for the Allies. The French produced a synchronised machine-gun of the same type while the British, with the assistance of a Romanian engineer named Constantinesco, developed an hydraulically-operated system which proved better than the mechanical in the long run.

In addition to the machine-guns designed mainly for the monoplane fighters, there were also those for the use of observers and in bombers. These included the British twin-Lewis and the German Parabellum, a light version of the Maxim.

Bombers

The first man to drop bombs on a town was a German, Lieutenant Ferdinand von Hiddessen, who let go three over Paris on 30 August 1914. For some weeks, at six o'clock every morning, the French capital was visited by an enemy aircraft in the hope of breaking down the morale of the inhabitants. These attacks soon prompted the French to hit back and a Frenchman, Corporal Finck, became the first man to bomb a military target, the hangars of the air defence unit at Metz where he destroyed a Zeppelin and three *Taube* aircraft. From that time air raids continued and the Allies kept the upper hand.

At first the missiles were of the simplest; one of the types was a bunch of steel dart that were dropped on groups of men. The German newspapers boiled with indignation after an attack of this nature, the first it would appear, made by two Belgian Farmans.

The earlier types of bomb caused a number of accidents of their own side and they were put on one side along with the darts. Next, the dropping of artillery shells was tried, such as the 75 mm and the 155 mm. Serious air bombardment started on 30 October 1914, when eight French aircraft attacked Dixmude. Two days later, thirty-two bombs were dropped on the Kaiser's headquarters at Thielt. From then on, air raids built up. By December, as many as eighteen aircraft were taking part; in June 1915, twenty-three aircraft raided Karlsruhe and in August, sixty-two French planes struck at Dillingen. On the same day, a mixed force of British, French and Belgian aircraft dropped some four tons of bombs on the Forest of Houthulst where the enemy had dug in.

Both the British and the Germans made great advances in the technique of the manufacture of bombs. In Britain, right from the beginning of the War, research was carried out at the Royal Laboratory at Woolwich and at the Royal Aircraft Factory at Farnborough. The heaviest bomb

GERMAN AIR FORCE II

1. Albatross C-III (1916) — 2. Albatross D-III (1917) — 3. Albatross D-II (1916–17) — 4. Halberstadt D-II (1917) — 5. Junkers CL-I (1918) — 6. Incendiary bomb for use from airships: A, B, inflammable material; C, detonator sleeve — 7. Section through anti-personnel bomb — 8–9. Karbonit bombs, 4·5 kg and 50 kg — 10. The first type of bomb to be released from aircraft in the Balkan War of 1913 — 11. Aerial torpedo P.U.W., 1,000 kg (1916–18) — 12–13. Pilot Lieutenants (1915) — 14. Non-commissioned officer observer — 15–16. Pilot Lieutenant, wearing Lancer-style uniform

1

2

3

4

5

6

A

B

C

7

shrapnel   charge   striker   fin

safety pin

detonator

8

9

10

11

12

13

14

15

16

L.&F.FUNKEN

used during the War, one of 10 cwt, was produced by them. The most commonly-used bombs weighed 1 and 2 cwt.

In Germany, the earliest bombs were produced by the Artillery Proving Board, but they soon became obsolete. They were followed by a type known as Karbonit. Then a third type which were torpedo-shaped, appeared in 1916. These had tail-fins, which increased their speed and hence their penetrating power. They ranged in weight from about 30 lb to 1 ton.

PILOTS

The fighter pilots of the Great War acquired a fame that was never equalled by those of the Second World War; few of the latter are now remembered. The reason is that, although the spirit of the Great War lived on, the conditions under which their combats took place had changed. In the Second World War, the air duels were over in a few moments and were often fought at such a height that they could not be seen from the ground.

In the Great War, the aeroplane was still something of a novelty, a battle in the air had something of the spirit of a tourney in the Middle Ages about it. The aircraft itself offered a challenge and there were always men who would take it up.

The most famous fighter pilot in France was Georges Guynemer although, with only 54 'kills', he comes second to René Fonck. On one occasion, Guynemer was engaged with the German Ernst Udet when he saw that Udet's machine-guns had jammed, so he broke off the fight, waved to him and returned to base. The same thing happened to Charles Nungesser, third in the French list with 45 'kills' but it was an unknown German pilot who was chivalrous this time. Nungesser, badly wounded, returned to base and to hospital. The first on the French score sheet, René Fonck, had 75 'kills' to his credit. It has been estimated that he accounted for 127 enemy aircraft in all. Generally, he needed only four or five rounds to bring his opponent down.

Fonck died peacefully at the age of 59; Guynemer was killed in action at the age of 23 and Nungesser was lost flying the Atlantic in 1927.

Britain, too, had her heroes, such as Major Mannock who had 73 'kills', Lieutenant Bishop with 72, and the Naval Officer Raymond Collishaw, with 60. Of these, only the first was killed in action, in 1918, and his grave has never been found. Another hero who did not achieve so many 'kills' before his untimely death was Captain Albert Ball who won the DSO and two bars as well as a posthumous VC. He made 43 'kills' before he was hit in an encounter with von Richthofen's 'circus' and crashed. He was, to quote the *Dictionary of National Biography*, 'the greatest fighting pilot of the air service . . .'.

Germany, likewise, had many gallant pilots, of whom the most famous was Manfred von Richthofen, whom we have already mentioned. He was shot down in 1918 in circumstances that

GERMAN AIR FORCE III

1. Pfalz — 2. Rumpler C-IV — 3. Roland C-II — 4. Albatross D-V — 5. Fokker triplane Dr. I — 6. Roland D-IVb — 7. Albatross D-Va — 8. Hannover CL-IIIa — 9. Siemens-Schukert — 10. Fokker D — 11. Bird's-eye view looking forwards of the cockpit of a Rumpler: (a) petrol tank; (b) petrol gauge; (c) oil tank; (d) observer-bomber's seat; (e) pilot's seat; (f) joy-stick; (g) cog-wheel operating the control cables; (h) cables controlling the ailerons; (i) pedals controlling the rudder; (j) cables connecting with the rudder; (k) electrical apparatus; (l) oil pressure gauge; (m) bomb rack — 12. Bomb-aimer, fitted level with the floor of the aircraft with the bombs outside the fuselage — 13. Pilot (1916–18) — 14. Observer (1916–18)

have remained a mystery, after winning 80 fights against such men as the Britain, Major Hawker. Next to Richthofen came Ernst Udet, with 62 'kills'. Udet died during the Second World War, driven to suicide by Göering and Milch. After Udet came Erich Löwenhardt, with 53 'kills'. He died in an air collision in 1918.

The score sheet for the other countries follows:

Austria-Hungary:	Godwin Brumowski	40
	Julius Arigi	32
	Franke Linke-Crawford	30
Italy:	Francesco Baracca	34
	Silvio Scaroni	26
	Ruggiero Piccio	24
U.S.A.:	E. U. Rickenbacker	26
	Frank Luke, Jr.	21
	Raoul Luftbery	17
Russia:	A. A. Kazakov	17
	P. V. d'Arguéev	15
	A. P. Séversky	13
Belgium:	W. Coppens	37
	A. de Meulemeester	11
	E. Thieffry	10

GERMAN AIR FORCE IV

1. Siemens-Schukert R-III (1917) — 2. Pfalz D-XIII (1918) — 3. Zeppelin R-XIV (Note the position of the air-gunners) — 4. Phœnix (Austro-Hungarian service) — 5. Fokker D-IX (1918) — 6. Observer's badge (worn on breast-pocket) — 7. Pilot's badge (worn on breast-pocket) — 8–9. Pilots (1916–18) — 10. Observer, winter dress with muffler (1916–18)

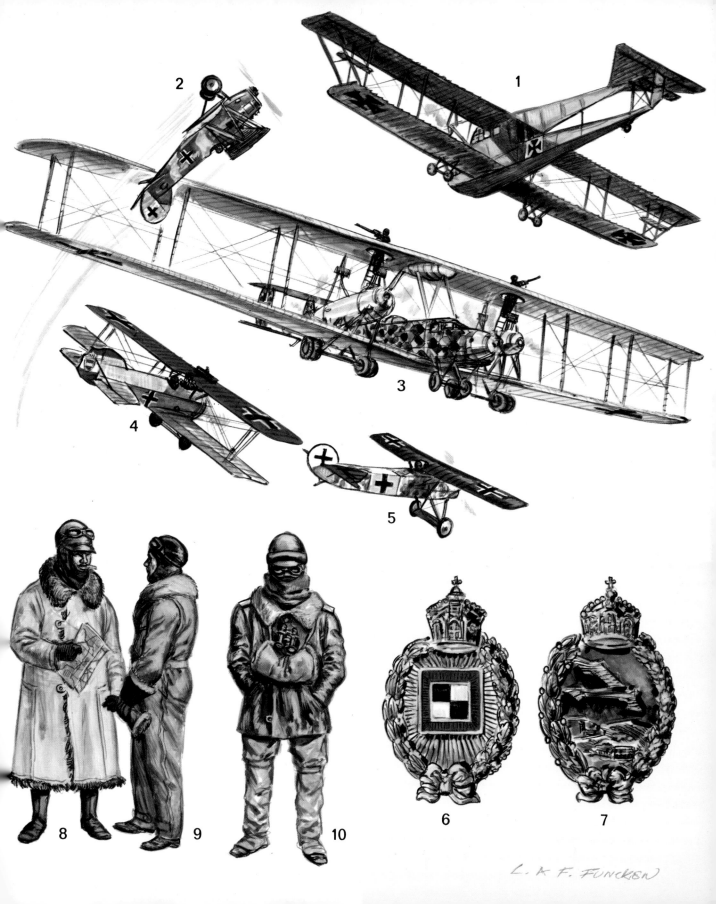

1

2

3

4

5

6

7

8

9

10

L. & F. FUNCKEN

Acknowledgements

The research involved in this vast and difficult subject has been as exciting as it has been arduous, and it has shown us, too, how wide the interest is and how anxious to help are the authorities in various countries, as well as our numerous friends and advisers. In particular, we wish to thank: the Curator and Dr G. Dirrheimer of the Heeresgeschichtliches Museum of Vienna, Brigadier A. I. Hulton M.B.E. of the Ministry of Defence and the Imperial War Museum, Lieutenant-Colonel Delay of the S.I.R.P.A., Captaine Petit of the Information Service for the Foreign Legion, Colonel Kashiwagi of the Japanese Embassy in Paris, Monsieur Leconte, Curator of the Royal Army Museum of Brussels and Monsieur Lorette, Curator of the *Cabinet des Estampes*.

We would also like to thank Rigo and F.G. Thompson and Roger Pierre, Pierre Louis, E. Kröner, Pierre Simon, J. Wagner, J. Dubois, R. Moulin, J. Courbet, P. Chayre, R. Alazet, J. Lesellier, W. Wilmotte, Commandant Bauman, J. Ernst, J. Lekeu, P. L. Gandini, F. T'Sas, D. de Pozdniakoff and Bastien.

List of Sources

Commandant Bucquoy — *Fanfares des Troupes à Cheval*
Brun, Charles — *Nos Soldats*
Calot, A. & C. Robert — *Les Uniformes de l'Armée Française*
Cary, J. — *Tanks and Armour in Modern Warfare*
Casberg, P. — *Deutschlands Armee*
Del Guidice, E. & V. — *Uniformi Militari Italiane*
Giglio, Vittorio — *Milizie ed Eserciti d'Italia*
Gurney, G. — *A Pictorial History of the United States Army*
Italiano, T. C. — *La Nostra Guerra 1915–1918*
Kerrigan, E. E. — *American Badges and Insignia*
Lamberton & Cheesman — *Fighter Aircraft 1914–1918*
Lavisse, Commandant — *Sac au Dos*
Melegari, Vezio — *I Grandi Regimenti*
Money Barnes, Major R. — *The British Army of 1914*
Munson, K. — *Fighters-Bombers 1914–1919*
Museum of Contempory
  History, Milan — *Dal Grappa a Vittorio Veneto*
Phelan, J. A. — *Heroes and Aeroplanes of the Great War 1914–1918*
Reich, A. — *Verdun*
Rottmann, H. — *Die Russiche Armee*
Ruhl, M. — *Die Uniformen der Deutschen Armee*
von Senger & Etterlin — *Kampfpanzer 1916–1966*
Smith, J. E. — *Small Arms of the World*
Tardieu, J. A. — *La Legion Étrangère*
Thiriar, J. — *Gloire et Misère*
Wanty, General E. — *L'Art de la Guerre*
White, B. T. — *German Tanks and Armoured Vehicles 1914–1945*
Zvegintsoff — *Uniformes de l'Armée Russe*

Almanachs Hachette 1915, 1916, 1917, 1918
Der Grosse Kreig in Bildern
Österreichische Militärische Zeitschrift
War Pictures
Revue de la Société Française des Collectioneurs de Figurines Historiques
Revue de la Société Belge d'Étude et du Costume 'La Figurine'
L'Illustration 1914–1918
Miroir 1914–1918
Panorama de la Guerre 1914–1918
Passepoil

Index

A

air force, Belgian 134
,, ,, British 134
,, ,, of Central Powers 136
,, ,, French 132
,, ,, Italian 134
,, ,, Russian 134
,, ,, United States 136
Albert I of Belgium 26, 32, 34
Alexander II of Russia 52
Alexeïev, General 58
arditi 64
Arisaka 82
armour, British 122–8
,, French 128–30
,, German 130
Army, Japanese 82–4
,, Polish 92
aviation 132–48
'Azor' 10

B

Ball 146
Bassi, Major 64
Beretta pistol 64
Bersaglieri 62, 64, 66, 68
Berthelot, General 88, 90
bombers 144
Botrel, Theodore 12
Brixia pistol 64
Broussilov, General 60, 86, 88
Browning 32
Byng, General 50

C

carabiniers (Belgian) 26, 28, 34
Carol I of Romania 86
chasseurs, German 94, 98
chasseurs alpins, French 12, 14
chasseurs à pied, Belgian 26, 28
,, ,, ,, French 10, 14, 18, 20
Collishaw 146
Colt 62
Constantine, King of Greece 80, 82
Croix de Guerre 20, 22
Currie, Sir Arthur 44

D

Desgouttes, General 34
Detaille, Edouard 10

E

Edward VII of England 36
Estienne, Colonel 128, 130, 138
expeditionary force, American 70, 76

,, ,, British 46
,, ,, Portuguese 76–8

F

Ferdinand I of Romania 86–90
forces, auxiliary (British) 44
,, Colonial 44
,, Dominion 44
,, Indian 44
Foreign Legion 14, 16, 24
Foch 48, 76
Fokker 136, 140
Fonck 146
fourragère 20, 22
Franchet d'Esperey 118
Franz Joseph III 112
French, Field Marshal 36

G

Gallieni, General 16, 48
Garros 140
gas-mask (Belgian) 28
,, (British) 42, 48
gendarmerie à pied (Belgian) 28
George V 36, 126
Glisenti pistol 64
godillots 10
Greece 80–82
grenade, disc 102, 106
,, French 20, 22–4
,, gas 102
,, ovoid 106
,, rifle 106
,, spherical 102, 106
,, stick 102, 106
grenade thrower 106
grenade, V. B. 22
grenadiers (Belgium) 26, 28, 34
,, (Russian) 52
Grossetti, General 32
Guards, Russian 52, 54
Guynemer 146

H

Hawker 148
helmet, Adrian 20, 40, 60, 78, 80, 88
,, British 40
Hotchkiss 24, 28, 84, 126, 130

I

infantry, Alpine (France) 14
,, of the Army of Africa
  (France) 14, 16, 24
,, Austro-Hungarian 108–12
,, Belgian 26–35

,, British 36–51
,, Bulgarian 118–21
,, Colonial 14, 16, 18, 20, 24
,, French 10–25
,, German 94–107
,, Italian 62–70
,, Light 10
,, Romanian 86–90
,, Russian 52–61
,, Serbian 78–80
,, Turkish 114–17

J

Joffre, General 16

K

Kaiser (Wilhelm II) 36, 80, 86, 94, 96
Kitchener, Lord 36, 48, 126
Kövess, General 80

L

Lanzerac, General 16
Lawrence, Colonel 116
Lebel rifle 12, 14, 24, 54, 102
Lee-Enfield rifle 46
Légion d'Honneur 20, 22
Legion, Pilsudski 92
Legion, Polish 92
Lenin 60
Lewis 40, 42
Ludendorff 56

M

machine gun, Austrian 108
,, ,, British 42
,, ,, French 22, 24
,, ,, German 100, 102
machine gunners, German 100, 102
machine guns, Italian 62
,, ,, Japanese 84
Mannlicher 88, 108, 112, 118
Mannlicher-Carcano 62
Mannock 146
March, General 76
Marines, French 32
Marne, Battle of the 58
Masaryk, Thomas 92
Mauser 26, 72, 76, 102, 114
Maxim 28, 64, 102
Médaille Militaire 20, 22
Montenegro 80
Mosin-Nagant 54
Mussolini 68
Mustafa Kemal (Atatürk) 116

N

Nambu 82, 84
Neuville, Alphonse de 10
Nicolas I 80
Nicholas, Grand Duke 58
Nungesser 146

P

Pan-Germanism 94, 96, 112
Pasha, Abdul Karim 116
Pasha, Enver 114
Pershing, Major-General 70
Pétain 50
Peter, King 80
Pickelhaube 96, 98, 100
pilots 146
Plumer, General 34
Putnik, General 78

R

reconnaissance 138
regiments, line, Belgian 26, 28, 34
    ,,   ,, French 10, 12, 14, 18, 20
    ,,   ,, Italian 62
    ,,   , Scottish 40
Renault 128
Renault, Louis 130
Rennenkampf 56, 58
Revelli 64
rifle, Austrian 108
  ,, Belgian 26
  ,, British 38
  ,, French 12, 24
  ,, German 102
  ,, Italian 62
  ,, Russian 54

Rommel 88
Ronarc'h Brigade 32

S

Saint-Chamond 128
Samsonov 56
Schneider 128
Schwarzlose 64, 108, 112
Somme, Battle of the 16
soutache 18
Springfield rifle 70, 72
St. Etienne 64
Steyr pistol 110
Swinton 124, 126, 128

T

Tamaquini, General 76
Tank Corps 122
Tannenberg 56
Territorials, French 12
tirailleurs, French 14, 16, 24
    ,, sénégalais 14, 18
Townshend, General 116
trench warfare 16
Triple Alliance 62
turcos (France) 14

U

Udet 146, 148
uniform, American 72–4
    ,,   Austrian 108
    ,,   Belgian 34
    ,,   British 38, 40, 42
    ,,   French 18–22
    ,,   German 98–100
    ,,   Italian 62
    ,,   Japanese 82

    ,, Russian 54

V

Vickers 40, 42, 126
Victoria, Queen 36
volunteers, British 46
    ,,   Czechoslovak 92
    ,,   Polish 92
von Bülow 48
von Falkenhayn 48
von Frittwitz 56
von Hindenburg 56, 58
von Kluck 48
von Mackensen 80, 88
von Moltke 48, 96
von Richthofen 142, 146
von Sanders 116
von Schlieffen 96

W

web equipment 38
Webley pistol 40
whippet 124, 128
Wilson (Woodrow) 70

Y

yeomanry 46
York, Corporal 74, 76
Ypres, Battle of 16
Yser, Battle of the 16, 32

Z

Zeppelin 136
zouaves (France) 14, 16, 24

L. & F. FUNCKEN